11+
& SATS
SPELLING
and
VOCABULARY

Advanced Level

Book Eleven

Stephen C. Curran

and

Warren Vokes

edited by Mark Schofield

This book belongs to:

....

Accelerated Education Publications

Exercise 228a

1) During their **conversation** he mentioned his brother's boat.

2) There was an old family _Photograph_ printed in sepia on the mantelpiece.

3) She had no _consideration_ of returning the ring after he ended their engagement.

4) _Conversation_ boys used to ride red motorcycles to deliver the messages.

5) "Solve the anagram and make a well known _phrase_ or saying."

6) They are very Green and, on _______________ , always buy recyclable products.

7) The best _national_ football teams contest the World Cup every four years.

8) She sings soprano in the church _choir_ and her husband is a tenor.

9) A _______________ of skill and good fortune enabled him to win the final.

10) It was a _fatal_ mistake that cost him dearly.

Score / 10

Exercise 228b

11) "Open the windows please: we need some _ventilation_ in here!"

12) He sold his opponent a dummy by managing not to _______________ the move.

13) Canterbury _cathedral_ is one of the oldest Christian structures in England.

14) Farm animals and pets are known as '_domestic_ animals'.

15) Some of the players were a little too _physical_ and the referee warned them.

16) "He is always _______________ : you could set your watch by him!"

17) A cross _section_ of the community had been asked to complete a questionnaire.

18) The issue under _intention_ in tonight's programme is truancy.

19) He was _continually_ interrupting and heckling the speaker.

20) Her revelations on television caused a _conversation_ .

Score / 10

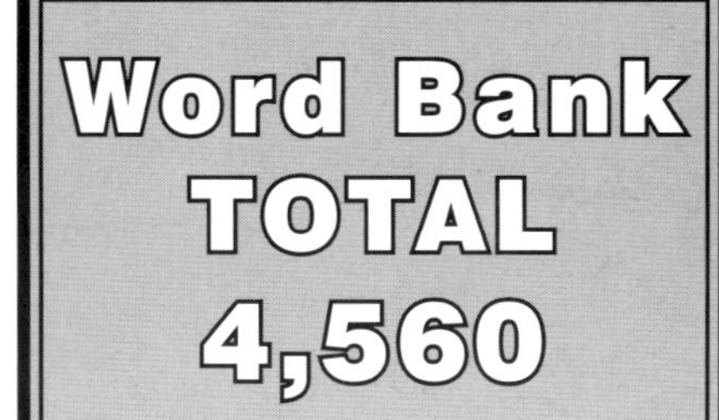

Across

228

1. The movement or circulation of fresh air.
3. A picture produced by a camera.
7. A physical feeling caused by having one or more of the sense organs stimulated.
9. Relating to or used in the home or everyday life within a household.
11. A distinct part that can be separated or considered separately from the whole of something.
12. Causing, or capable of causing death.
13. A message sent by telegraph.
14. A string of words that form a grammatical unit.
16. Existing in the real world and able to be touched and seen.
18. A mixture of different things or factors.
19. An informal talk with somebody.

Down

2. Something that somebody plans to do or achieve.
4. Arriving or taking place at the arranged time.
5. A church that contains a bishop's throne and is the most important church in the bishop's diocese.
6. Happening again and again.

Down (continued)

8. Thoughtful concern for, or sensitivity towards, the feelings of others.
10. A long-distance communication method through wires.
14. An important underlying law or assumption.
15. Relating or belonging to, or representing a nation as a whole.
17. An organized group of singers.

Put the mystery letter (✱) into the box marked **228** below. Add in the mystery letters from puzzles **229** to **234** then rearrange them to make **Dickens's Mystery Word**.

The clue is:
COMMUNICATIONS

228	229	230	231	232	233	234

Mystery Word:

Now rearrange them:

Score

20

Across

229

3. A condition that affects what happens or how somebody reacts in a particular situation.
6. Showing great bravery, courage, or determination.
7. An absolute ruler who exercises power cruelly and unjustly.
8. A single thing in a group or collection of things.
14. Experiencing serous lack of contentment or happiness.
15. The parts of the earth between or near the tropics of Cancer and Capricorn.
17. Greatly impressive in appearance.

Across (continued)

18. Somebody who is qualified to fly an aircraft or spacecraft.
19. Help given or made available to another.
20. Possessing a large skeletal structure and having strong muscles.

Down

1. Having a pleasant or sweet smell.
2. Having no occupant or contents.
4. To take hold of an object quickly and firmly.
5. Stylishly graceful, and showing sophistication and good taste in appearance or behaviour.
9. Somebody who rents a building, house, set of rooms, plot of land, or some other piece of property for a fixed period of time.
10. Financial protection against loss or harm.
11. Characterized by spending excessively or wastefully.
12. A small short-barrelled gun designed to be held in one hand.
13. The act or process of remembering people, things, or events.
16. An excellent or perfect example of something or somebody, or something that is considered a perfect example.

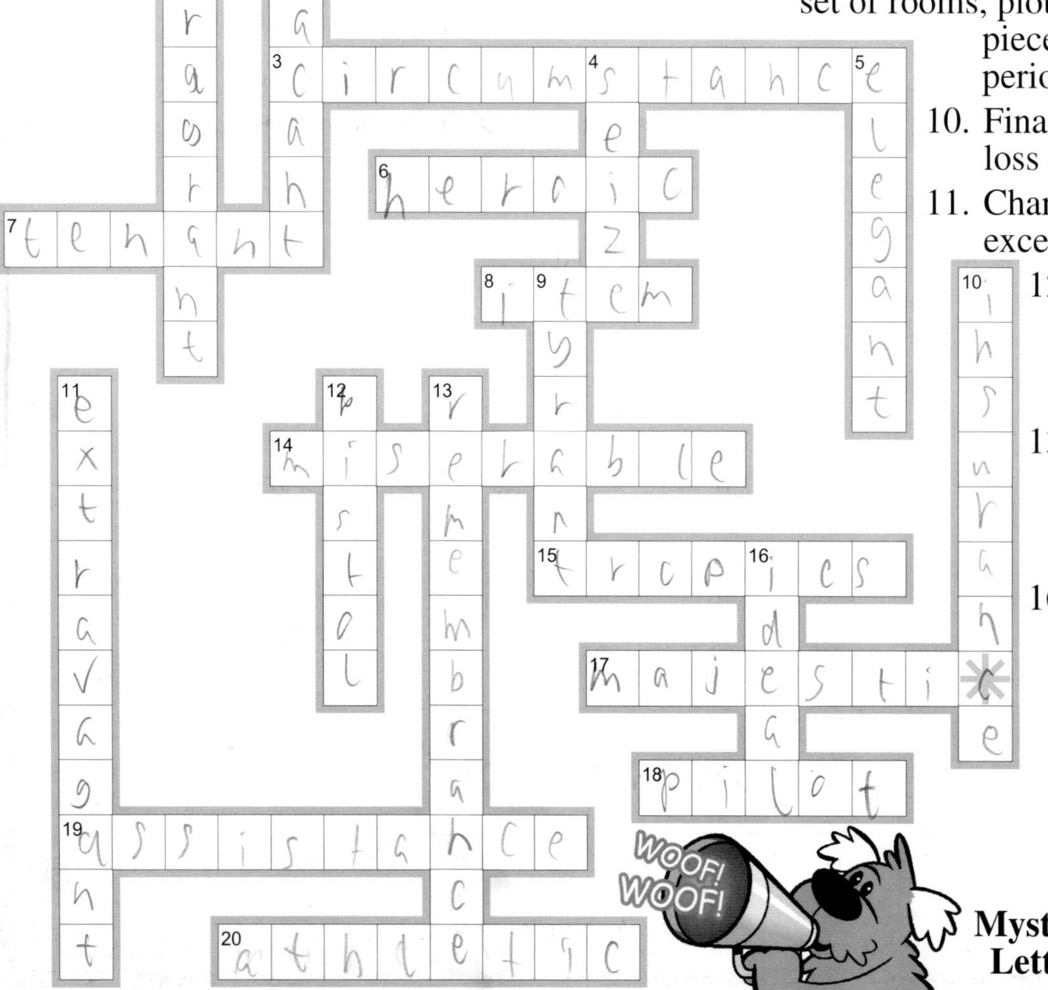

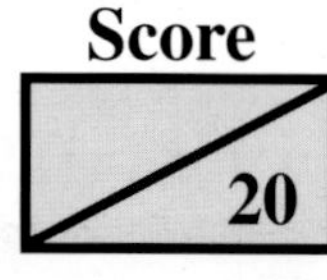

Mystery Letter

Score

20

4

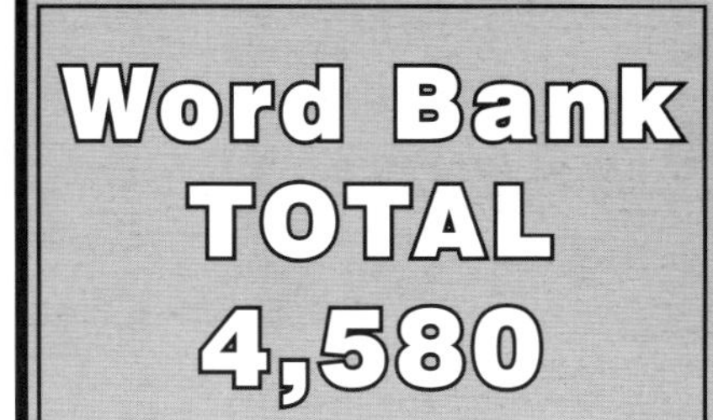

Exercise 229a

1) She put up a __heroic__ fight against her cancer but finally she succumbed.

2) It is a __majestic__ seascape showing the masts of twenty tall ships under full sail.

3) "Never hesitate : __seize__ any opportunity and use it to your advantage!"

4) The ship slowed as it neared the coast to take on board a __pilot__ .

5) He lived a __miserable__ existence, struggling from day to day just to survive.

6) Before her holiday in the __tropics__ , she began a course of anti-malaria tablets.

7) He was a __tyrant__ and stood trial for his crimes against humanity.

8) She checked her shopping list: there was one __item__ that she still had to buy.

9) The fire produced __extravagant__ quantities of smoke but very little heat.

10) She drew a small __pistol__ from her handbag and fired it.

Score 10

Exercise 229b

11) It was pure __circumstance__ that he just happened to be present at the time.

12) She screamed in horror and several people came to her __assistance__ .

13) A service of __remembrance__ is held on the Sunday closest to 11th November.

14) His __vacant__ look indicated that he had no idea of the answer to her question.

15) She is an __elegant__ lady, always immaculately dressed and neatly coiffured.

16) He has an __athletic__ build with superb muscle tone and a deep tan.

17) "I recommend that you take out __insurance__ against loss or damage."

18) The __tenant__ asked his landlord to have the storm damage repaired.

19) In an __ideal__ world there would be no war, no fear and no hunger.

20) The lilies have a __fragrant__ scent that pervades the room.

Score 10

Exercise 230a

1) The report stated that the _probable_ cause of the accident was driver fatigue.

2) "Stay away from him: he's a bad _influence_ on you."

3) It is an enormous car supermarket selling cars of every _description_ .

4) The highest level of _cleanliness_ is essential to prevent infection.

5) She was called as a _witness_ for the prosecution at her former employer's trial.

6) The column looked far from vertical when viewed from a different _angle_ .

7) A fitter came to _convert_ her appliances from town gas to natural gas.

8) "I'll _probably_ be there this afternoon but I haven't yet finally decided."

9) The _destruction_ of Hiroshima by an atomic bomb was horrific.

10) The food was _reasonable_ but the service was poor.

Score 10

Exercise 230b

11) The land is low-lying and _liable_ to flood when it rains heavily.

12) The sustained period of very cold weather caused an _energy_ crisis.

13) He called his mother to express his _concern_ about his father's ill health.

14) What he earned seemed a _trifle_ beside his mountain of debts.

15) His car was always breaking down, so he traded it in for a more _reliable_ one.

16) "Don't _despair_ . Although it seems hopeless, there's always a solution."

17) "The Union has _muscle_ and can protect its members from exploitation."

18) His actions were well-meant but _capable_ of being misinterpreted.

19) Newspapers _despise_ politicians who abuse their power and position.

20) A new pipeline was built to _convey_ crude oil to the refinery.

Score 10

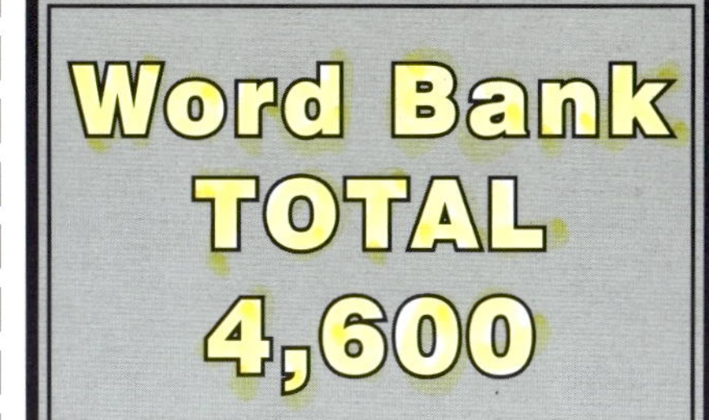

Across

230

2. As is likely or to be expected.
5. A profound feeling that there is no hope.
6. The act or process of destroying something.
9. A reason to worry, or something that causes worry.
11. To change the nature or form of something, or to be changed in nature or form.
14. The degree to which somebody keeps clean or a place is kept clean.
16. Likely to experience or do something, often something unpleasant or hazardous.
17. Something that has little or no importance, significance, or value.
18. The effect of something on a person, thing, or event.

Down

1. Likely to exist, occur, or be true, although evidence is insufficient to prove or predict it.
3. A figure formed by two lines diverging from a common point.
4. To look down on and feel contempt for somebody or something.
7. Somebody who saw or heard something that happened and gives evidence about it.
8. Sensible and capable of making rational judgments.
9. To take somebody or something somewhere.
10. A written or verbal account, representation, or explanation of something.
12. Able to be trusted to do what is expected or has been promised.
13. A tissue that is specialized to undergo repeated contraction and relaxation, thereby producing movement of body parts.
14. Good at a particular task or job or a number of different things.
15. Liveliness and forcefulness.

Mystery Letter

Score

20

Across

231

5. A feeling or expression of opposition.
6. Teaching in a particular subject or skill, or the facts or skills taught.
9. A drug or remedy used for treating illness, especially in liquid form.
11. The receiving of something given or sent.
12. Something that gives a sign or proof of the existence or truth of something, or that helps somebody to come to a particular decision.
13. An action prohibited by law.
16. Having the qualities or value claimed.
18. A period during which somebody is away.
19. A strong feeling of wanting to be successful in life and achieve great things.
20. The process of mentioning or alluding to somebody or something.

Down

1. A severe shortage of food resulting in widespread hunger.
2. The house, flat, or other dwelling in which somebody lives.
3. A group of travelling entertainers, including clowns, acrobats and sometimes animal trainers and their animals.
4. The feeling of pleasure that comes when a need or desire is fulfilled.
7. To formally signal respect to another member of the armed forces or to a flag.
8. Precise and distinct in describing the limits of something.
10. Something done or a way of behaving that is not genuine but is meant to deceive other people.
14. A coarse-grained igneous rock made up of feldspar, mica, and at least 20 per cent quartz.
15. The physical existence of somebody or something in a particular place.
17. An official who supervises play and enforces the rules of the game in some sports.

Mystery Letter

Score

20

© 2006 Stephen Curran

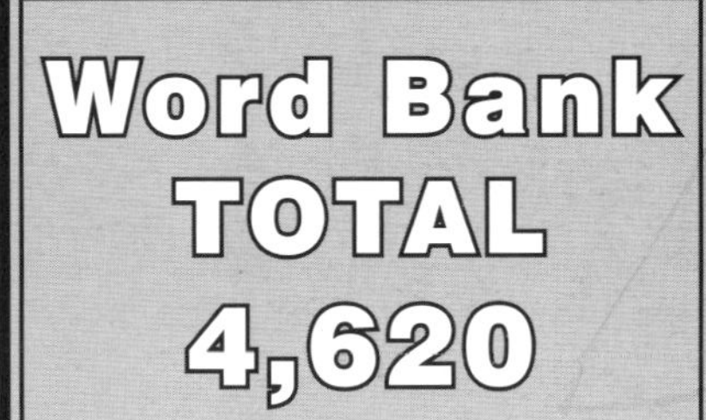

Exercise 231a

1) The statue of Eros, the god of love, stands in Piccadilly _circus_   circus

2) After an _absence_ of over five years, the band had a record in the charts.

3) "I might be able to go too: I'll give you a _definite_ answer tomorrow."

4) Her _ambition_ is to become a leading gynaecologist in a teaching hospital.

5) He seemed an affable and _genuine_ person who would fit in well with the others.

6) The UN peace-keeping troops maintained a heavy _presence_ in the city.

7) The town was gripped in a _crime_ wave with a significant increase in burglaries.

8) She located the directory in the _refrence_ section of the local library.

9) He could no longer keep up the _pretence_ and admitted that he had lied.

10) The _umpire_ overruled the linesman and called the ball 'out'. **Score** 10

Exercise 231b

11) He received a written _instruction_ to rent the property for his client.

12) Mormon pioneers quarried massive _granite_ blocks to build the Salt Lake Temple.

13) She had no _objection_ in principle but doubted the wisdom of the proposal.

14) The signal is weak and _reception_ is poor on this television channel.

15) The archeologists sifted the soil for _evidence_ of Roman remains.

16) The new recruit failed to _salute_ the officer and was rebuked by the sergeant.

17) 'Chequers' is the official country _residence_ of the serving Prime Minister.

18) He chose a career in _medicine_ to enable him to care for sick people.

19) The _famine_ is widespread and many could die before aid arrives.

20) The mystery was never explained to my _satisfaction_. **Score** 10

9

Exercise 232a

1) "I'm sorry to __disappoint__ you, but I shan't be joining you on the trip."

2) The river was __swollen__ after the heavy rain and likely to burst its banks.

3) The monks of the ______________ made mead from honey to sell to the public.

4) The barrister was keen to __acquaint__ the jury with the facts surrounding the case.

5) It is an exact replica with all the intricate __detail__ faithfully reproduced.

6) Jesus was able to __distribute__ five fishes and two loaves among 5,000 people.

7) The __burden__ of proof always rests with the prosecution in a trial.

8) He is an old __acquaintence__ whom she has not met since their school days.

9) Elizabeth I finally decided to __execute__ her cousin, Mary, Queen of Scots.

10) The tensile __strength__ of cast iron is negligible.

Score | 10

Exercise 232b

11) They expressed their __gratitude__ to the staff by making a donation to the hospice.

12) She was not well __acquainted__ with her husband's side of the family.

13) He placed the film into the tray of chemicals and watched it slowly __develop__ .

14) She left a __deposit__ and returned later to collect and pay for the bracelet.

15) The families were __destitute__ and dependent on charity.

16) She spent many years studying the migration __pattern__ of swallows.

17) He made his fortune as an entrepreneur and now lives a life of __luxury__ .

18) Countless failures served only to __strensthen__ his resolve to succeed one day.

19) She lived in France for a year to __acquire__ fluency in the language.

20) "I can't hear. Turn up the __volume__ please."

Score | 10

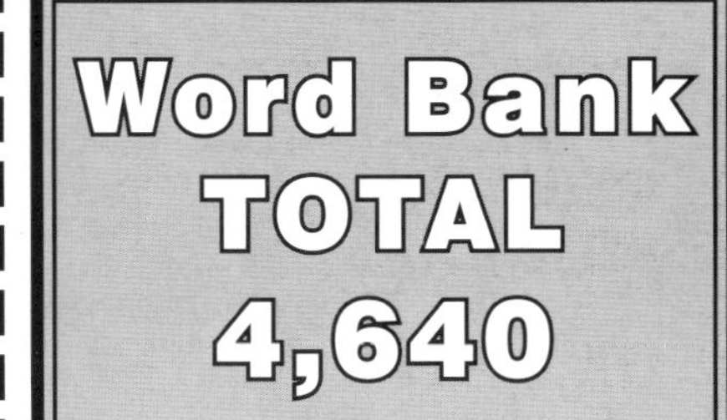

Across

232

3. The physical power to carry out demanding tasks.
4. To get or obtain possession of something.
5. Made larger, fuller, or rounder, or expanded in size or shape.
9. A feeling of being thankful to somebody for doing something.
11. To deliver or share things out to people.
12. To put an instruction or plan into effect.
14. A repeated decorative design, for example on fabric.
16. To make somebody, or yourself, aware of or familiar with something.
17. An individual separable part of something, especially one of several items of information.

Across (continued)

18. To be less good, attractive, or satisfactory than was hoped or expected.
19. The size of a three-dimensional space enclosed within or occupied by an object.

Down

1. To put or drop something somewhere.
2. Somebody who is known slightly rather than intimately.
6. An activity that gives great pleasure, especially one only rarely indulged in.
7. To change, or cause to change, and become larger, stronger, or more impressive, successful, or advanced.
8. To make something stronger or more powerful, or increase in strength or force.
10. Having some, often not very much, knowledge of something.
11. Lacking all money, resources and possessions necessary for subsistence.
13. A building or buildings occupied by monks under an abbot or nuns under an abbess.
15. A load being carried.

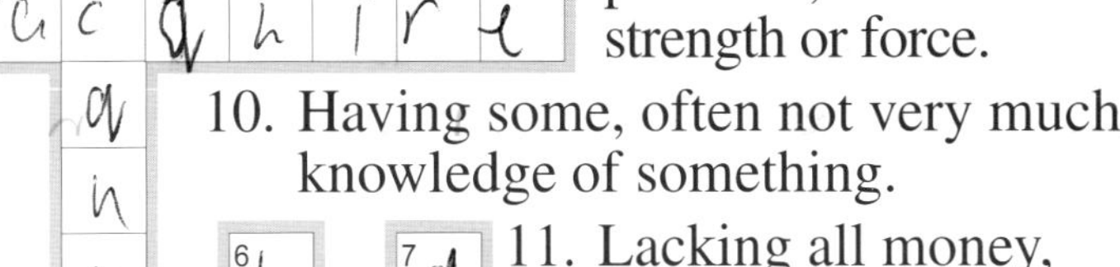

Mystery Letter E

Score 20

Across

233

2. A formal and usually written request for something.
4. To plan and make something in a skilful or artistic way.
5. To redirect something that strikes a surface, especially light, heat, or sound.
7. An identifiable or distinctive quality of food or drink perceived with the combined senses of taste and smell.
10. To hurt somebody's feelings, or cause resentment, irritation, anger, or displeasure.
12. Somebody who is on a journey to a particular place or who uses a particular form of transport.
13. To set free a person or animal who is imprisoned, trapped, or confined in some way.
14. Something said or written in reply to a statement or question from somebody else.
17. To give up a paid or unpaid post voluntarily.
18. The part of something that is left after other parts have gone or been used up.
19. To be against something or to take an active stance against something.

Down

1. To have a favourable opinion of somebody or something.
3. Somebody who carries a message or messages between people.
6. To invite somebody to participate in a fight, contest, or competition.

Down (continued)

8. An actively hostile attitude towards something, or a resistant stance against something.
9. To keep something back for future use or for some specific purpose.
10. To subject a person or a people to a harsh or cruel form of domination.
11. An institution of higher or further education.
15. On the side that faces something or at the furthest distance possible from something.
16. To disclose something that was unknown or secret.

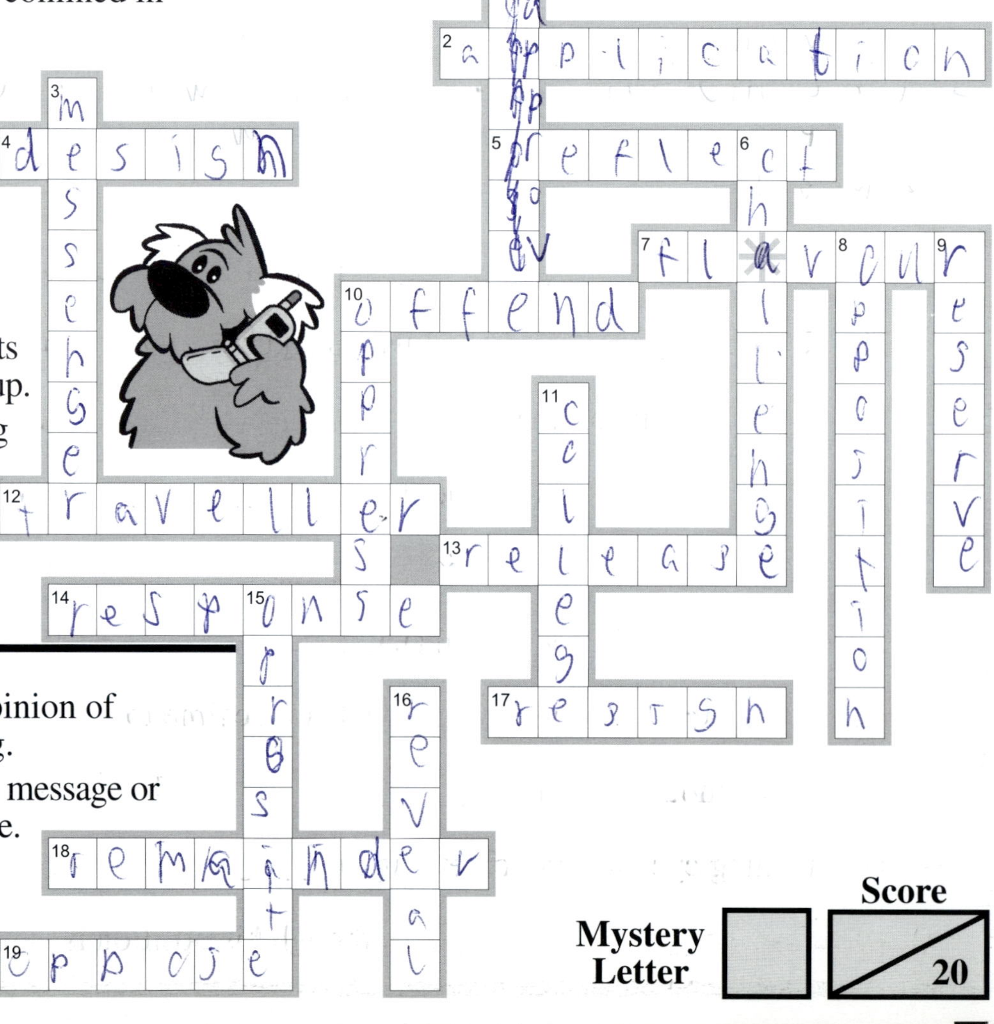

Mystery Letter

Score

/20

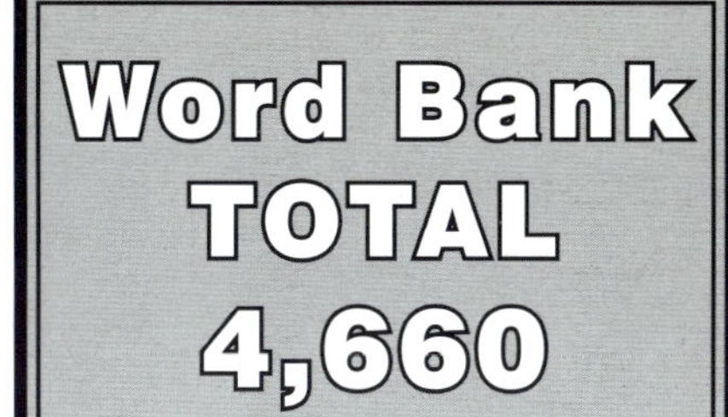

Exercise 233a

1) She completed and returned the job _application_ form.

2) The car salesman removed the cover to _reveal_ the latest model.

3) Her parents _approve_ of her decision to apply for a place at university.

4) The anti-vivisection group would not state openly that they _oppose_ violence.

5) He is a seasoned _traveller_ who has visited over fifteen countries.

6) The _College_ of Cardinals sat to deliberate and elect a new Pope.

7) Public _opposition_ to the proposed development was growing.

8) The sailor threw the _messenger_ line to the dock worker on the quay.

9) Many of the members _offend_ against the club's strict dress code.

10) She waited for a _response_ but he remained silent. **Score** ☐ 10

Exercise 233b

11) It has an unusual _flavour_ , rather like aniseed with a hint of mint.

12) The elegant _design_ of the wings and body gave *Concorde* a graceful appearance.

13) "I think you should sit there quietly and _reflect_ on your misconduct."

14) He took out the £1 coins and put the _remainder_ of his change in a jar.

15) The foreman handed over to his _opposite_ number on the next shift.

16) The company's public relations manager handed a press _release_ to the journalists.

17) The conquering army implemented a harsh regime to _oppress_ the population.

18) The sentry shouted out a _challenge_ : "Halt! Who goes there? Friend or foe?"

19) The winning cyclist kept something in _reserve_ for the sprint finish.

20) He refuses to _resign_ even though his position is untenable. **Score** ☐ 10

Exercise 234a

1) He replied to the _advertisement_ in the newspaper and bought the item.

2) She visited her mother every Saturday and _occasionally_ during the week too.

3) He suffers from emphysema and has been an _invalid_ for many years.

4) Her insurance company required an _independent_ assessment of the damage.

5) The steam pipe had fractured and a cloud of water _vapour_ filled the room.

6) He decided to _yield_ control of the company to his daughter and retire.

7) An _enormous_ crowd waited outside the palace to cheer the royal couple.

8) She used a fork to _pierce_ the pastry before placing the pie in the oven.

9) The waitress poured a _generous_ amount of cream onto the gateau.

10) "You must _practise_ playing the piano every day".

Score 10

Exercise 234b

11) It began as a _rumour_ but by lunchtime everyone believed it to be the truth.

12) The children found it hard to contain their _excitement_ as Christmas drew near.

13) One child in the class was _impudent_ and showed no regard for the teacher.

14) He passed an _innocent_ remark but she misunderstood and turned on him.

15) He is a _mischievous_ child, always playing pranks and teasing people.

16) She raised her hand to _shield_ her eyes from the sun's glare.

17) He tried without success on _numerous_ occasions to beat his sister at tennis.

18) It was _marvellous_ to see his family again after living abroad for five years.

19) "Don't _advertise_ that the house is empty by forgetting to cancel the milk.

20) He carries a compass but never has _occasion_ to use it.

Score 10

advertise   **advertisement**
practise   **impudent**
yield   **shield**
pierce   **invalid**

Across 234

3. Showing a lack of respect and excessive boldness.
6. To penetrate through or into something with a sharp pointed object.
8. To publicize the qualities of a product, service, business, or event.
10. A gaseous substance.
13. Extraordinarily wonderful.
14. Not guilty of a crime or offence.
15. Free from authority, control, or domination.
16. Having or showing a willingness to give money, help, or time freely.
19. Behaving or likely to behave in a naughty or troublesome way, but in fun and not meaning serious harm.
20. Not acceptable or correct because of being based on a mistake or employing flawed reasoning.

Down

1. The amount of something, especially a crop, produced by cultivation or labour.
2. Many in number.
4. The feeling or condition of lively enjoyment or pleasant anticipation.
5. Now and then.
7. The act of advertising something.
9. Unusually large or great in size, amount, or degree.
11. To do something repeatedly in order to improve performance.
12. A particular time.
17. A piece of armour carried on the arm.
18. A generally circulated story, report, or statement without facts to confirm its truth.

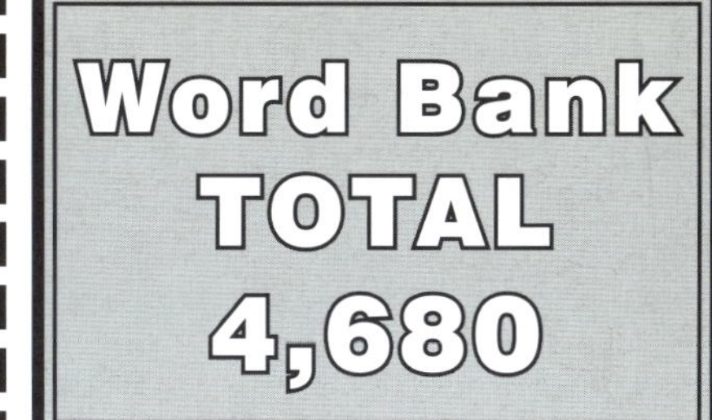

Don't forget to go back to page **3** and complete **Dickens's Mystery Word.**

Mystery Letter

Score / 20

At the Birthday Party

Can you find all these words in the picture below? Write the correct word against each number. When you have finished you can colour in the picture if you want to.

candles	entertainer	card	doll	balloons
slice	presents	jelly	patch	blindfold
donkey	lemonade	fairy cake	zip fastener	éclair

1. _slice_
2. _balloons_
3. _patch_
4. _donkey_
5. _lemonade_
6. _jelly_
7. _presents_
8. _fairy cake_
9. _card_
10. _zip_
11. _doll_
12. _candle_
13. _éclair_
14. _blindfold_
15. _entertainer_

On the Canal

Can you find all these words in the picture below? Write the correct word against each number.

painter	lifebelt	landing net	lock	narrowboat
duck	railing	fender	hamper	bait
fishing rod	lock keeper	stern	reel	bow

1. _lock_
2. _railing_
3. _bait_
4. _landing net_
5. _bow_
6. _painter_
7. _life belt_
8. _fender_
9. _reel_
10. _stern_
11. _fishing rod_
12. _duck_
13. _narrow boat_
14. _lock keeper_
15. _hamper_

Put the mystery letter (✱) into the box marked **235** below.
Add in the mystery letters from puzzles **236** to **242** then rearrange them to make **Oliver's Mystery Word**. The clue is:
CLOTHING

Across

235

3. The view somebody takes about a certain issue.
6. To make somebody feel angry or exasperated.
9. A container that gives a shape to a molten or liquid substance poured into it to harden.
11. Eagerness to do something immediately.
14. Having advanced cultural and social development.
15. To articulate sounds or words.
16. With a very cold temperature.
18. The controlling of something or the managing of the way it works.

Down

1. The innermost being or nature of somebody.
2. The ability to process food in the body.
4. Annoyed by being kept waiting.
5. To announce something publicly or formally.
7. To pledge devotion or dedication to somebody or something.
8. A thing that somebody has created, especially a device or process.
10. To think about something and come to understand or appreciate what it means.

Down (continued)

12. To go on to do something.
13. Somebody who is being given medical treatment.
14. Polite, but in a way that is cold and formal.
15. Domestic fowl in general raised for meat or eggs.
17. Somebody who is the legal inheritor of something.

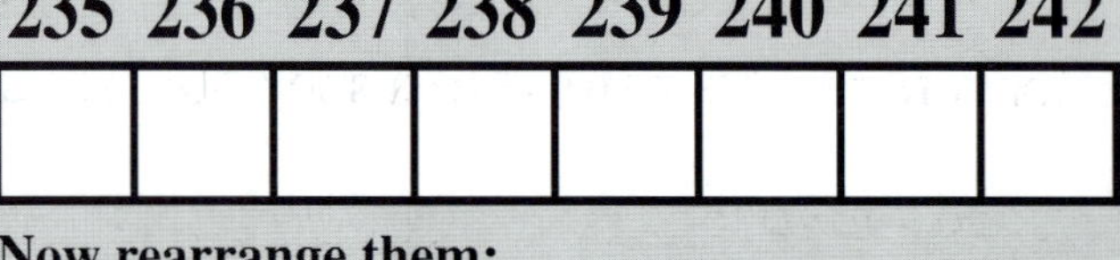

235 236 237 238 239 240 241 242

Now rearrange them:

Mystery Word:

Score

20

18

© 2006 Stephen Curran

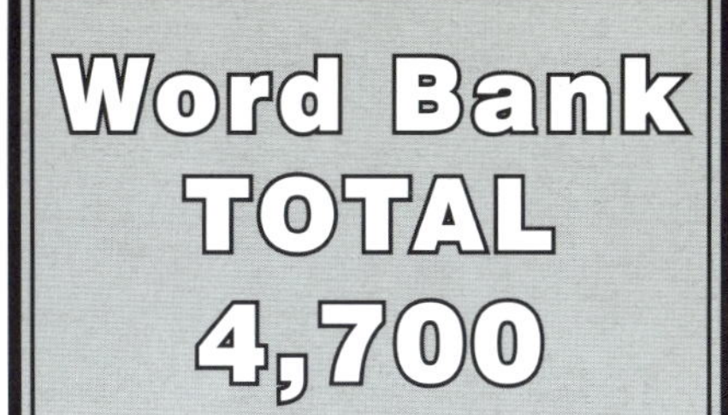

Exercise 235a

1) His story is pure ___________________ and bears little or no relation to the truth.

2) Our generation is the unfortunate __heir__ to decades of pollution.

3) Her childhood experience helped __mould__ her personality.

4) He received a very __frigid__ reception and wished he had not come.

5) She used the opportunity to __proclaim__ her innocence before she was imprisoned.

6) The Dunkirk evacuation in 1940 was a huge military and naval __operation__ .

7) He is a __patient__ man: exceedingly slow to anger and tolerant to a fault.

8) She used her frailty to __provoke__ sympathy from her captors.

9) The police did not prosecute the culprit, so the victims began a __civil__ action.

10) "All his __poultry__ is free range: he detests battery farming."

Score ___ / 10

Exercise 235b

11) He extracted the salient points from the paper and presented them in a __digest__ .

12) He could no longer contain his __impatience__ : he had to *do* something.

13) "I now __pronounce__ you man and wife." proclaimed the registrar.

14) She acted in a __civilized__ way, showing the utmost courtesy and respect.

15) The crowd cheered as they watched the parade __proceed__ along the route.

16) The electorate were __impatient__ for change and voted in a new government.

17) He is able to __commit__ intricate details to memory and recall them perfectly.

18) The doctor referred his patient to a specialist for a second __opinion__ .

19) "Stress is bad for your __digestion__ : it causes stomach ulcers."

20) It is dull, repetitive, __soul__-destroying work.

Score ___ / 10

commence   recommend   recollect
shipping   comrade   complaint
humour   endeavour   tobacco
pension   provision   decision

Exercise 236a

1) Sir Walter Raleigh introduced _tobacco_ to England in the 16th Century.

2) She went to the doctor with a _complaint_ and he prescribed her medication.

3) The Prime Minister asked the Queen to _dissolve_ parliament.

4) Advances in forensic science have enabled police to _solve_ more crimes.

5) She married a _shipping_ magnate whose company owned a huge fleet .

6) His team finished top of their _division_ and won promotion.

7) Attempting the climb was a heroic _endeavour_ but he failed to reach the summit.

8) "If you continue to _annoy_ me with that whistle, I'll take it away from you!"

9) The _decision_ to turn back, due to the bad weather, proved to be right.

10) Many families in poorer regions still live in _poverty_ .

Score: 10

Exercise 236b

11) Ill-health forced her to retire from work and to claim a disability _pension_ .

12) The film has little to _recommend_ it other than its special effects.

13) "Can you _recollect_ what your daughter was wearing?"

14) The constant sound of barking dogs _annoyed_ him intensely.

15) The enquiry into the incident found that he alone was _wholly_ responsible.

16) The young recruit was proud that the older soldiers regarded him as a _comrade_ .

17) At the _conclusion_ of their negotiations, both parties signed the agreement.

18) "I know he can be demanding but just _humour_ him to keep the peace."

19) The performance is scheduled to _commence_ at 8.30 pm.

20) No _provision_ has been made for non-ambulant visitors.

Score: 10

Across

236

1. The act of supplying or providing something.
4. Harassed or bothered somebody repeatedly.
9. A statement expressing dissatisfaction with something.
11. To begin happening or to begin something.
12. Somebody who is either a close friend or a companion.
13. Totally and in every way or to the fullest extent.
14. To become absorbed in a liquid solution, or cause this process to occur to a solid.
16. The act or business of transporting goods.
18. To make an effort to achieve something.

Across

19. To find a way of dealing successfully with a problem or difficulty.
20. A decision made or an opinion formed after considering the relevant facts or evidence.

Down

2. To bring something back to mind.
3. To suggest something as worthy of being accepted, used, or done.
5. The quality or content of something that elicits amusement and laughter.
6. A plant whose large leaves are dried and processed primarily for smoking.
7. To make somebody feel impatient or angry.
8. The state of not having enough money to take care of basic needs.
10. Something that somebody chooses or makes up his or her mind about, after considering it and other possible choices.
15. The act of separating or splitting something into parts, or an instance of this.
17. A fixed amount of money paid regularly to somebody during retirement.

Mystery Letter

Score / 20

mutiny   variety   society
sacrifice   margin   origin
original   moral   crystal
transform   translate   character

Across

5. A clear, colourless mineral, especially quartz.
6. Existing first, from the beginning, or before other people or things.
9. To change people or things completely.
10. To bring somebody or something into existence.
11. Delicate and pretty.
12. The largest of the three sovereign nations that make up the Iberian peninsula.
13. To satisfy a thirst by drinking something.
15. The reaching of a place after coming from another place.
16. With a charming, old-fashioned quality.
18. A starting point or first cause.
19. The set of qualities that make somebody or something distinctive.

Down

1. A plan of action.
2. To give an equivalent in another language for a particular word or phrase.
3. A blank space on the left or right edge, or at the top or bottom, of a written or printed page.
4. A rebellion against legal authority.
7. A snack or light meal usually made with two slices of bread with a filling in between.
8. A structured community of people bound together by similar traditions, institutions, or nationality.
12. A symbolic offering made to a god.
14. The quality of being varied or diversified.
17. A conclusion about how to behave or proceed drawn from a story or event.

Mystery Letter

Score 20

22

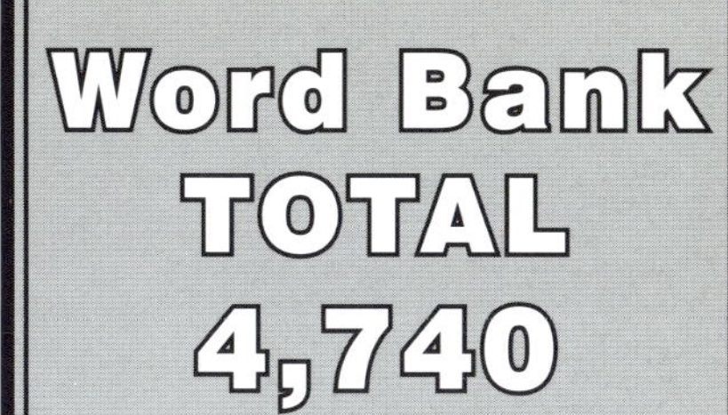

Exercise 237a

1) Work began to _transform_ the wasteland into a children's playground.

2) The firemen played water from their hoses onto the blaze to _quench_ the flames.

3) He had act quickly: travelling at that speed left no _margin_ for error.

4) The _sandwich_ course provided a perfect balance between work and study.

5) The _mutiny_ on HMVA *Bounty* in 1789 was led by Fletcher Christian.

6) ETA, a terrorist group in _Spain_ , is attempting to achieve Basque independence.

7) The staff quickly became bored due to the lack of _variety_ in their work.

8) "He is a _quaint_ old man whose dress, speech and manners are from the 1940s!"

9) She studied the cast list in the _programme_ before the play began.

10) The _original_ drawings were lost but exact copies still exist. **Score** / 10

Exercise 237b

11) Hydraulics _translate_ the pressure of a finger into powerful movement.

12) She wore a _dainty_ pair of slippers trimmed with lace.

13) "After days of heated discussions their _arrival_ at an agreement seems unlikely."

14) He played Malvolio, the pompous _character_ in Shakespeare's *Twelfth Night*.

15) The rights of women in modern _society_ have been supported by legislation.

16) He proposed that the committee _create_ a new category of 'life member'.

17) She had to _sacrifice_ her rook to his queen to enable her to gain the advantage.

18) He looked on the internet for the _origin_ of the idiom *"as pleased as Punch"*.

19) The fortune teller peered into her _crystal_ ball to predict the future.

20) They won a _marginal_ victory but were not awarded damages. **Score** / 10

Exercise 238a

1) Many young people decide to ___emigrate___ and seek their fortune abroad.

2) She cut up the food to make it more ___manageable___ for her young son.

3) The wind blew in from the northeast making it feel ___extremely___ cold.

4) She played a ___creditable___ rendition of Christian Sinding's *Rustle of Spring*.

5) The riders tried to catch and overtake each other in the cycling ___pershit___ .

6) He arrived at an ___intellegent___ solution by applying his mind to the problem.

7) Paper making, the compass, gunpowder, and printing are all ___chinese___ inventions.

8) St. Paul's Cathedral is the ___supreme___ example of Sir Christopher Wren's skill.

9) An ___obstinate___ blockage in the waste pipe resisted all attempts to clear it.

10) He lacked ___suitable___ footwear for the muddy conditions. **Score** / 10

Exercise 238b

11) Although happily married, she continued to ___mourn___ the loss of her independence.

12) Switzerland, since declaring itself neutral, has remained a ___peaceable___ country.

13) Prohibition was an ___extreme___ measure enforced by the 18th Amendment in 1920.

14) He left his well-paid job to ___pursue___ his ambition to care for the homeless overseas.

15) The company introduced a training ___scheme___ to improve productivity.

16) The hat she wore at Ascot was an amazing ___creation___ that turned people's heads.

17) "Trust the British weather to ___interfere___ with our plans for a trip to the seaside!"

18) At the end of his service, he left the army with an ___honourable___ discharge.

19) He was a British ___emigrant___ who had moved to Australia in the 1950s.

20) She found a reliable ___source___ who confirmed the rumour. **Score** / 10

extreme   extremely

scheme   pursue

pursuit   mourn

source   intelligent

Across

238

1. Inclined towards peace and avoiding contentious situations.
5. The bringing of something into existence.
6. The place where something begins.
7. Able to be handled or controlled without much difficulty.
10. Above all others in power, authority, rank, status, or skill.
14. Somebody who leaves a place to go and live in another country.
15. To meddle in the affairs of other people.
17. Determined not to agree to other people's wishes or accept their suggestions.
18. A group of related languages spoken across most of China.
19. To follow or chase somebody in order to catch, overtake, or attack him or her.

Down

2. To a very high degree.
3. Having intelligence, especially to a highly developed degree.
4. To feel and show sadness because somebody has died.
8. To leave a place, especially a native country, to go and live in another country.
9. Bringing credit or worthy of praise.
10. A secret and cunning plan, especially one designed to cause damage or harm.
11. The effort made to try to achieve or obtain something over a period of time.
12. Guided by, or with a reputation for having, strong moral and ethical principles.
13. Of the right type or quality for a particular purpose.
16. Highest in intensity or degree.

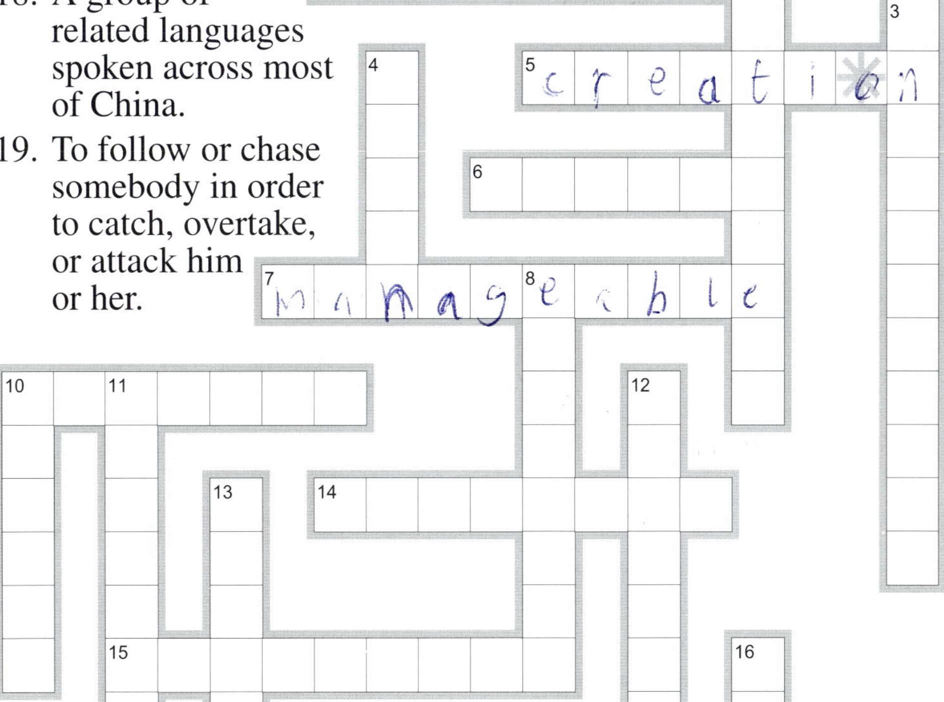

Mystery Letter

Score

20

Oliver's Page of Knowledge
Inventors and Inventions

Trevor Bayliss (7)
Clue: This man's invention is powered by a constant velocity spring. It enables people who have no access to mains supply electricity or replacement batteries to keep in touch with news and world events.

John Logie Baird (10)
Clue: He was born in Helensburgh, Argyle, Scotland in 1888. The first public demonstration of his invention of image transmission was in the Selfridge's department store in London in 1926.

Rudolph Diesel (9)
Clue: In 1892 he invented a propulsion system in which the fuel is ignited by being suddenly exposed to the high temperature and pressure of a compressed gas. He intended to use a variety of fuels including coal dust.

Laszio Biro (2)
Clue: He was a Hungarian journalist who, after noticing that the ink used in printing newspapers dried quickly, invented in 1938 this revolutionary writing implement.

Charles Babbage (3)
Clue: He was the first to conceptualize and design a fully programmable version as early as 1820, but the device was never actually constructed in his lifetime.

Inventor		Invention
1. __________________	invented	__________________
2. __________________	invented	__________________
3. __________________	invented	__________________
4. __________________	invented	__________________
5. __________________	invented	__________________

**Safety Match · Jet Engine
Television · Clockwork Radio
Ballpoint Pen · Diesel Engine
Pneumatic Tyre · Plough
Computer · Spinning Jenny**

Gustaf Erik Pasch ❹
Clue: In 1844 this Swede invented a safer version of an earlier invention of 1836. His invention used red instead of white phosphorous and separated the combustible ingredients until the product was used.

Robert William Thomson ❽
Clue: In 1845 this Scotsman patented the Aerial Wheel. His invention was only applied to horse-drawn carriages but was later re-invented to be used on bicycles.

Frank Whittle ❺
Clue: On 16th January 1930, in England, he submitted patents for his own design of a device that now powers aircraft all over the world. It was granted in 1932.

Joseph Foljambe ❶
Clue: He developed the first commercially successful version of this implement in 1730. It was made from iron with a mouldboard that would cut, lift and turn over the strip of earth.

James Hargreaves ❻
Clue: In about 1764 his invention revolutionised the cotton trade. His device dramatically reduced the amount of work needed to produce yarn, with a single worker able to work eight or more spools at once.

Inventor		Invention
6. _____________	invented	_____________
7. _____________	invented	_____________
8. _____________	invented	_____________
9. _____________	invented	_____________
10. _____________	invented	_____________

Exercise 239a

1) The rules state that the panel's _________________ is final.

2) From the top of the hill on a cloudless day the view is _________________ .

3) The grey _____________ was introduced into England and South Africa from America.

4) The _________________ has been superseded by the computer and word processing.

5) The survey revealed that the floor could not _____________ the weight of the machine.

6) Governments around the world gather _________________ about each other.

7) The hunter tracked his _____________ for several miles before sighting it.

8) He sent an email to _________________ her on passing her driving test.

9) _________________ debated the bill in an all-night sitting and rose at 5.30 am.

10) "I still _________________ that he knew that the notes were forged." **Score** /10

Exercise 239b

11) The guttering had fractured and a _____________ of rainwater cascaded down the wall.

12) Their homework was to write an _____________ entitled *The Merits of Mediocrity*.

13) His calmness and _________________ indifference to the situation surprised his parents.

14) The decor is _____________ and ostentatious with overuse of gilt and garish colours.

15) The Cuban missile crisis in 1962 was a major international _________________ .

16) The *Mona Lisa* is arguably the most famous _____________ in Western art history.

17) His off the cuff remarks caused great _____________ and he apologized unreservedly.

18) He dictated an important letter for his secretary to __________ and post immediately.

19) They had a _________________ of opinion but soon resolved it amicably.

20) The doctor gave her a _________________ examination. **Score** /10

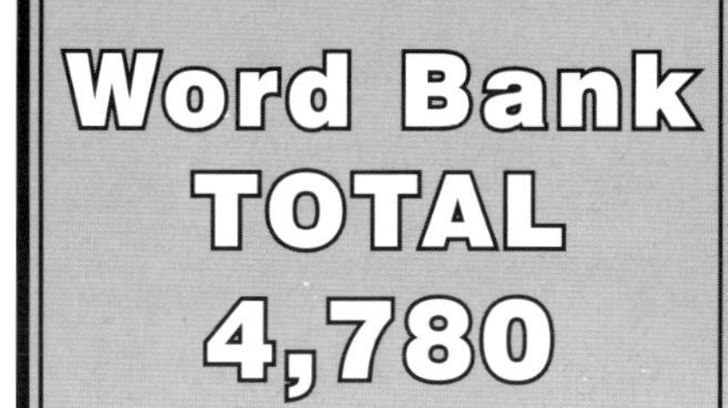

Across

239

1. The intellectual skill or knowledge of somebody.
3. The quality of being different from or unlike something or somebody else.
5. The decision arrived at and pronounced by a court of law.
9. Extremely careful and accurate in doing something.
11. A short piece of written work set as an assignment for a student.
14. To make a situation or course of action continue in the same way as before.
16. Something said to express praise and approval.
18. Clearly seen or understood.
19. An electrical or mechanical device for printing words on individual sheets of paper.

Across (continued)

20. A category of things or people whose members share some qualities.

Down

2. A fast and powerful rush of liquid, especially water.
4. Crude or obscene.
6. Beautiful, impressive, and splendid in appearance.
7. A painting, photograph, or drawing of somebody, somebody's face, or a related group.
8. A nation's legislative body, made up of elected and sometimes non-elected representatives.
10. An official crime, or a crime against moral, social, or other accepted standards.
12. A small bushy-tailed rodent that lives in trees and eats nuts and seeds.
13. Something that happens, especially a single event.
15. To manage to withstand something and continue doing something in spite of it.
17. An open excavation from which stone or other material is extracted by blasting, cutting, or drilling.

Mystery Letter

Score

/20

Across

240

1. A European songbird that lays its eggs in the nests of other birds.
5. A female writer of a book or other text.
8. Extremely tired or weak.
10. A tool for cutting and shaping wood or stone.
12. Consistently trustworthy and loyal, especially to a person, a promise, or duty.
14. A shape like a stretched circle with slightly longer, flatter sides.
17. The sport of catching fish with a hook, line, and rod.
18. Goods or cargo carried by a commercial means of transport.
19. A room or building to live in.

Across (continued)

20. A game similar to tennis using rackets to strike a shuttlecock back and forth across a high net.

Down

2. Caused by a lack of courage, or lacking courage.
3. A small bomb designed to be thrown by hand and detonated by a time fuse.
4. Potentially dangerous to human beings or the environment.
6. To damage somebody's dignity or pride, especially publicly.
7. Islands, often small ones.
9. Cutting and preparing boneless portions of fish, poultry or meat.
11. To change liquid into a vapour.
13. The place to which somebody or something is going or must go.
15. Something that assures a particular outcome.
16. Socks, stockings, and tights, considered collectively.

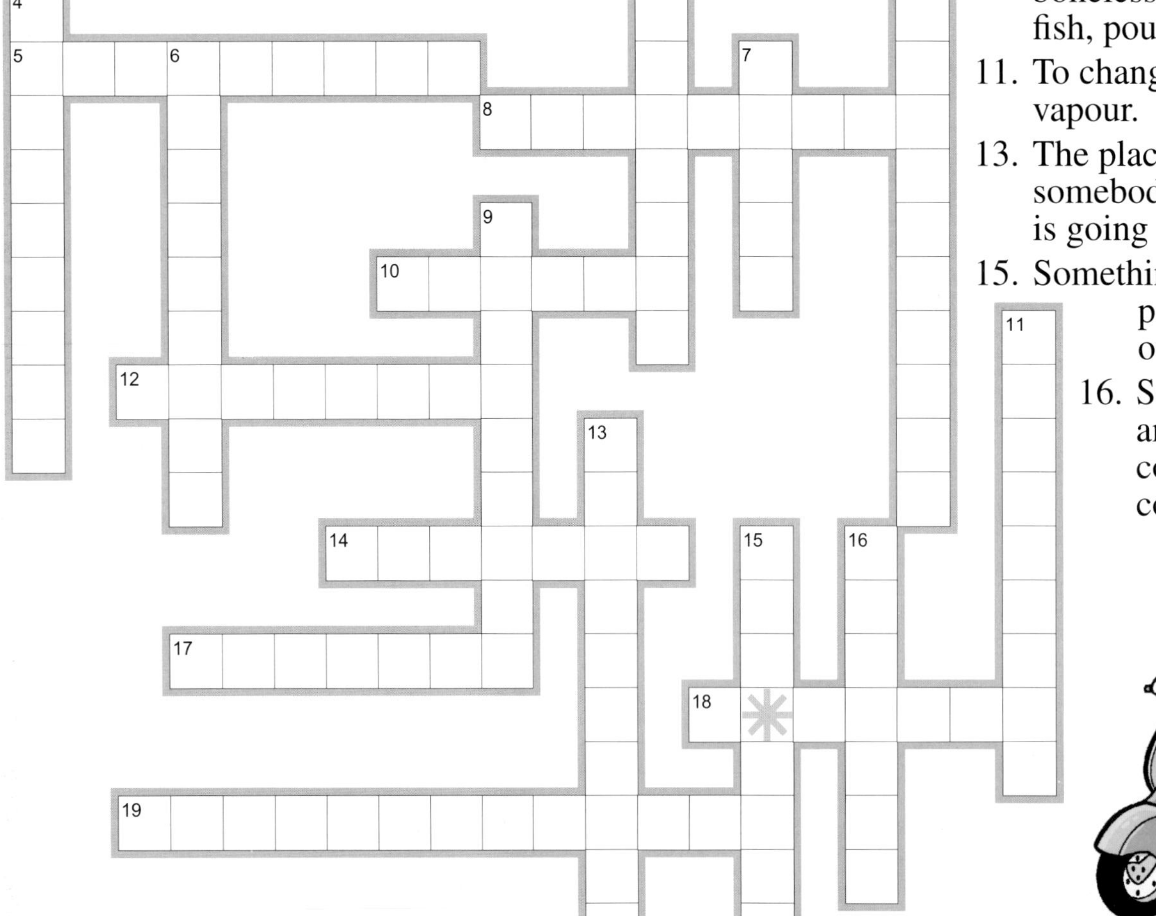

Mystery Letter

Score

20

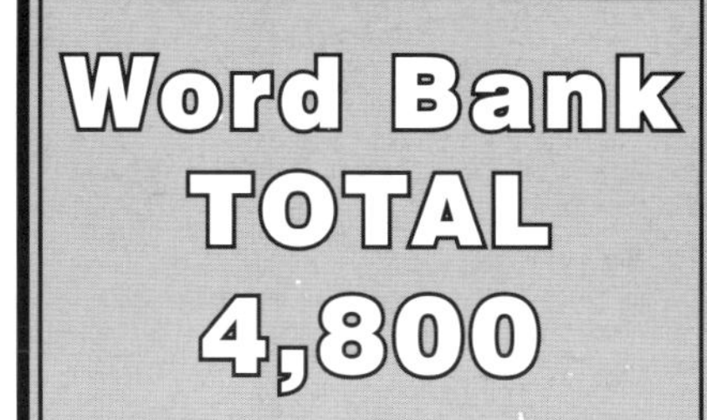

Exercise 240a

1) The mine is fully worked out and the coal seams are _________________ .

2) He was _____________ his presentation towards a more mature audience.

3) With their _________________ only a few kilometres further on, their pace quickened.

4) The Mills bomb was the first modern fragmentation _________________ .

5) She took her _________________ racket to the sports shop to have it restrung.

6) She is a successful _________________ but writes under a male nom de plume.

7) The sculptor studied his maquette and began to ___________ the stone.

8) A rugby ball is shaped like an ____________ to make it easier to carry and handle.

9) The _________ of Scilly form an archipelago of islands off the Cornish coast.

10) The waiter stood by their table _____________ the Dover sole.

Score /10

Exercise 240b

11) The mist slowly began to _________________ once the sun broke through.

12) The journalist submitted a _____________ account of the events to his editor.

13) They heard the two-note call of the _______________ from deep within the woods.

14) She bought two pairs of socks, and four pairs of tights in the _____________ department.

15) He could not _________________ them seats for tomorrow afternoon's flight.

16) She rang the Post Office to set up an _________________________ address.

17) A chemical spillage can be extremely _________________ to the fire brigade.

18) He asked if the company could ___________ the parts by air in order to save time.

19) Robbing the old lady was a _______________ and despicable act.

20) She would _________________ him by ridiculing him in public.

Score /10

Exercise 241a

1) A vending machine dispenses coffee and other hot ___________________ .

2) The ______________ is the headquarters of the United States Department of Defense.

3) The ballet class learnt how to ________________ on one foot with their arms held aloft.

4) At the end of the evening the ___________________ shared out their tips.

5) The tourists were entertained by ________________ dancers wearing grass skirts.

6) Visitors to Britain are often surprised to find our policemen so ______________ .

7) The Royal ___________________ , Greenwich was commissioned in 1675.

8) A gypsy dancer shook her ___________________ and struck it with her hand.

9) He was fined and had his licence endorsed for ________________ the speed limit.

10) The women had __________ all day and were extremely tired.   **Score** 10

Exercise 241b

11) The workhouse master used a ________ to serve gruel from the copper to Oliver Twist.

12) His father had a shy and managed to knock off and win a ________________ .

13) The club's supporters are ________________ about their football team and hate to lose.

14) "When the stock market _____________ I'll consider selling some of my shares."

15) Real __________ is the original racket sport from which the modern game originates.

16) __________ is played on a square board of eight rows (ranks) and eight columns (files).

17) The Opposition tried to ___________________ the Government Minister's reputation.

18) The pilot was forced to make an ___________________ landing when an engine failed.

19) The internal angle at each vertex of a regular _______________ is 135°.

20) He trained the Border ____________ to be an excellent sheepdog.   **Score** 10

Across   **241**

1. A game played on a chequered board by two players, each with 16 pieces representing a king and his attendants.
7. A spoon with a long handle and a deep bowl.
8. Recovers or improves after a setback, crisis, or period of illness, inactivity, or deterioration.
11. A fruit consisting of a hard fibrous husk surrounding a single-seeded nut with a firm white flesh and hollow core containing sweet-tasting liquid.
13. A fast complete spin of the body.
16. An unexpected and sudden event that must be dealt with urgently.
17. A shallow, single-handed drum with jingling metallic discs in its frame.

Across (continued)

18. Worked long and hard.
19. A geometrical figure that has five sides and five angles.

Down

1. A dog with a long narrow muzzle, originally bred to herd sheep.
2. To kill somebody, especially a political leader or other public figure, by a sudden violent attack.
3. Going beyond the limits of something in quantity, degree, or scope.
4. A Polynesian or Hawaiian dance.
5. Excessively enthusiastic about a particular belief, cause, or activity.
6. A building, station, or artificial satellite used for scientific observation of natural phenomena.
9. A game played on a rectangular court by two, or two pairs of, players with rackets who hit a ball back and forth over a net.
10. Women who bring food or drink to tables.
12. Drinks other than water.
14. Willing to be helpful or do favours.
15. A closed plane figure that has eight sides and eight angles.

Mystery Letter

Score / 20

Exercise 242a

1) After all the ___________________ , the opening night had finally arrived.

2) The bed-sit was equipped with a small ___________________ in one corner.

3) The taller the ___________________ , the more prestigious the company.

4) He supplied his publisher ___________________ with chapters of his novel.

5) She stood in the wings acting as ___________________ for the actors on stage.

6) Ships and planes have mysteriously disappeared inside the Bermuda ___________________ .

7) At the end of extra time it was a draw, so the match was decided on ___________________ .

8) Her house was just above the high water line and was___________________ by the flood.

9) The powdered ________ remains part of the official attire of an English barrister.

10) She replaced the toner ___________________ in the laser printer.

Score | 10

Exercise 242b

11) Nowadays, a waterproof ______________ is a standard in military field uniforms.

12) His astrological telescope is mounted on a ___________ for stability.

13) Professional golfers employ a ___________ to carry their bag of clubs and to assist them.

14) At the clinic, her baby had an ___________________ against measles, mumps and rubella.

15) The wingspan of the great ___________________ is the largest of any bird.

16) ______________ are often progenitors in allergies and allergic reactions to certain foods.

17) The athlete's performance reached a ______________ and ceased to improve.

18) Two dummy chimneys maintained the building's ___________________ appearance.

19) Special ______________ rates applied for visitors from overseas.

20) The Latinised symbol for the Japanese ________ is ¥.

Score | 10

rehearsals	cartridge
albatross	penalties
caddy	inoculation
Yen	kitchenette

Across

242

1. A modern building that is extremely tall.
7. A hill or mountain with a level top.
8. A simple outer garment for the body in the form of a single piece of heavy cloth, often wool, with a slit in it for the head.
10. A covering of hair, or something resembling hair, worn on the head for adornment.
11. Legal or official punishments.
14. A frame or stand with three legs.
16. Sincere and genuine, with no intention to mislead or deceive.
17. A large long-winged seabird that inhabits cool southern oceans and spends most of its life in flight.

Across (continued)

18. A container for liquid or powder that is loaded into a device.
19. Having both sides of a central dividing line correspond or be identical to each other.

Down

2. A unit of Japanese currency.
3. Food sources that are rich in protein molecules.
4. A very small room, or part of another room, fitted out as a kitchen.
5. Somebody who visits places away from home for pleasure.
6. Somebody in a theatre whose job is to provide the missing words for actors who have forgotten their lines.
8. Little by little.
9. A small box or tin used for storing something, especially tea.
12. A plane figure that has three sides and three angles.
13. The injection of a serum, into somebody's body to create immunity to a disease.
15. A series of sessions in which something that is to be done later is practised.

Mystery Letter

Score

/20

In the Garage Workshop

mechanic	spanner	wheels	jack	chain
cylinder	bonnet	heater	hoist	toolbox
battery	exhaust	spark plug	axle stand	screwdriver

1.______________________ 2.______________________ 3.______________________

4.______________________ 5.______________________ 6.______________________

7.______________________ 8.______________________ 9.______________________

10.______________________ 11.______________________ 12.______________________

13.______________________ 14.______________________ 15.______________________

In the Butcher's Shop

Can you find all these words in the picture below? Write the correct word against each number.

knives	cash register	mincer	chops	slicer
turkey	pies	joints	scales	pasties
butcher	cleaver	sausages	burgers	saw

1.____________________ 2.____________________ 3.____________________

4.____________________ 5.____________________ 6.____________________

7.____________________ 8.____________________ 9.____________________

10.____________________ 11.____________________ 12.____________________

13.____________________ 14.____________________ 15.____________________

heal
serving
cenotaph
leveret

professional
roulette
glider
skiing

tourniquet
antiseptic
encouragement
ukelele

Across

243

2. A monument erected as a memorial to a dead person or dead people buried elsewhere.
3. To become or cause to become shrunken or wrinkled.
5. An agent that prevents or reduces infection.
10. An instrument like a small guitar with four strings.
14. A young hare.
15. Alone.

Across

17. Support of a kind that inspires confidence and a will to continue.
18. A gambling game with a spinning wheel.
19. The activity, sport or pastime of travelling on skis.

Down

1. Waiting on customers in a shop.
3. A fabric square worn by women over the shoulders, or head and shoulders, or used to wrap a baby in.
4. A tight encircling band applied around an arm or leg in an emergency to stop severe arterial bleeding.
6. A quiver or shudder.
7. A single expansion and contraction of an artery, caused by a beat of the heart.
8. Engaged in an occupation as a paid job rather than as a hobby.
9. An engineless aircraft.
11. Making a long and difficult journey, especially on foot.
12. Judged legally to be unable to pay off personal debts.
13. Suffering from or carrying a disease that can be transmitted by direct or indirect contact.
16. To make a person or injury healthy and whole.

Put the mystery letter (✳) into the box marked **243** below. Add in the mystery letters from puzzles **244** to **249** then rearrange them to make **Kate's Mystery Word**.

The clue is: **BEAUTY**

Mystery Word:

243	244	245	246	247	248	249

Now rearrange them:

Score

20

Exercise 243a

1) She usually sings _____________________________ but today she is with a band.

2 He declared himself _____________ and removed his burden of debt.

3) The casino welcomes gamblers and has tables for blackjack, _____________ and craps.

4) Unless they can _________ the rift in their party, they stand little chance in the election.

5) Impetigo is very _____________________ : many children in the class will be affected.

6) She booked a series of lessons with the _____________________ at the golf club.

7) The _____________ slipped the tow at 2,000 feet and banked sharply to starboard.

8) The fruit was old and had begun to _____________ in the warmth of the room.

9) George Formby strummed the _______________ and sang humorous songs.

10) A _____________ is born fully furred and with its eyes open.

Score / 10

Exercise 243b

11) The baby was christened wearing the ___________ that its mother had worn.

12) They stood on the touchline and shouted _____________________________ to the team.

13) He used his tie as a _____________________ in a desperate attempt to stop the bleeding.

14) The earthquake's _______________ was felt over fifty miles from the epicentre.

15) The nurse cleaned the wound with _________________ and applied a dressing.

16) They tried pony _______________ for the first time while on holiday in Wales.

17) Their _____________ instructor on the piste wore a red sweater and red woollen hat.

18) The Queen laid a wreath of poppies at the _________________ on behalf of the nation.

19) The player _______________ from the far end is a former Wimbledon champion.

20) The doctor felt her _______________ : it was slow and weak.

Score / 10

bachelor   headgear   propeller
aqualung   trophy   composer
overturn   estuary   bassoon
violence   thrive   overcoat

Across

4. Something worn on the head.
6. The remains of an animal or plant preserved from an earlier era inside a rock or other geological deposit.
7. A cup, shield, plaque, medal, or other award given as a token of victory, success, or other achievement.
11. To turn something upside down.
12. Somebody who writes music.
14. An electronic device that accepts, processes, stores, and outputs data at high speeds according to programmed instructions.
17. A book, play, or film that has an exciting plot involving crime, mystery, or espionage.

Across (continued)

18. A Native North American heelless shoe made of deerskin or other soft leather.
19. The sudden loud release of energy and a rapidly expanding volume of gas.
20. To grow vigorously and healthily.

Down

1. An unmarried man.
2. A telephone, or to call somebody on the telephone.
3. The wide lower course of a river where the tide flows in, causing fresh and salt water to mix.
5. The use of physical force to injure somebody or damage something.
8. A heavy coat worn over other outer clothes.
9. A low-pitched double-reed instrument of the oboe family.
10. A revolving shaft with spiral blades that causes a ship or aircraft to move by the backward thrust of water or air.
13. Somebody, especially a king or queen, who rules a state or territory, usually for life and by hereditary right.
15. Somebody whose job is to design buildings and advise on their construction.
16. An underwater breathing apparatus used by divers.

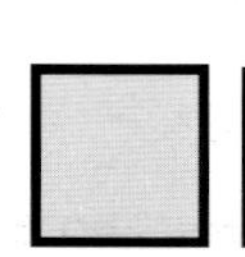

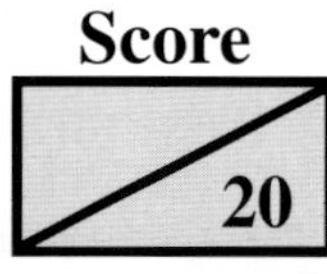

Exercise 244a

1) They stood on the stern and watched the wake made by the ship's _______________ .

2) Johann Sebastian Bach was a prolific German _______________ and organist.

3) She packed a copy of his latest _______________ to read on her holiday.

4) He had been a _______________ all his life and it was unlikely that he would marry now.

5) She plays _______________ in the woodwind section of the philharmonic orchestra.

6) He moved the shrub and it appeared to __________ in its new location.

7) She is a self-made woman and the _______________ of her own fortune.

8) They sailed down the river to the _____________ , where the tidal race was quite strong.

9) She switched on her laptop _______________ and logged on to the internet.

10) He took off his _______________ and carried it over his arm.

Score [/ 10]

Exercise 244b

11) Anti-royalists campaign to replace the _______________ with a president.

12) "I now call upon our guest speaker to present the ____________ to the winning team."

13) The storm's _______________ was extremely destructive, damaging buildings and vehicles.

14) He threaded the lace around the back of the _______________ and tied it at the front.

15) She left a voice-mail message asking him to __________ her when he got in.

16) It was a huge _______________ that left a pall of thick black smoke over the town.

17) Emile Gagnan and Jacques Cousteau developed the _______________ in 1942.

18) Their lawyer asked the Court of Appeal to _______________ the verdict.

19) Burning __________ fuels increases carbon dioxide emissions and pollution.

20) Boxers wear protective _______________ whilst sparring.

Score [/ 10]

confetti	offshore	throttle
conker	moonlight	arguable
graph	overcast	contest
untrue	pianist	overhead

Exercise 245a

1) The ship was too late to enter the port so it anchored ________________ until the morning.

2) He made a hole through the ______________ , then threaded and knotted the string.

3) The library books were _____________ and she was fined when she returned them.

4) The rioters built a ________________ of burning cars across the street.

5) They awoke to another _______________ day with little chance of sunshine.

6) The arrests resulted in the ________________ of large amounts of stolen property.

7) The race started: the motorcyclist opened the ______________ and raced into the lead.

8) Her paternal grandfather was Polish and her ________________ grandfather was Welsh.

9) The great pyramids built by the ancient Egyptians are truly ______________ .

10) The Russian spy planned to _____________ to the West.

Score / 10

Exercise 245b

11) He measured the ________ of the two concentric circles from their common centre.

12) The scout troop entered a team in the ____________ and finished in second place.

13) She returned the high ball with a powerful ________________ smash.

14) The ground outside the registry office was littered with colourful ______________ .

15) It's ______________ whether Andrés Segovia is the father of the modern classical guitar.

16) She collected all the data, then used a computer program to ___________ the results.

17) His command of the language is poor and the task of translating is ________________ .

18) The concert _____________ is a highly acclaimed virtuoso on the keyboard.

19) In the clear night air the ________________ reflected off the water's dark surface.

20) He was banished from England for being ____________ to the King. **Score** / 10

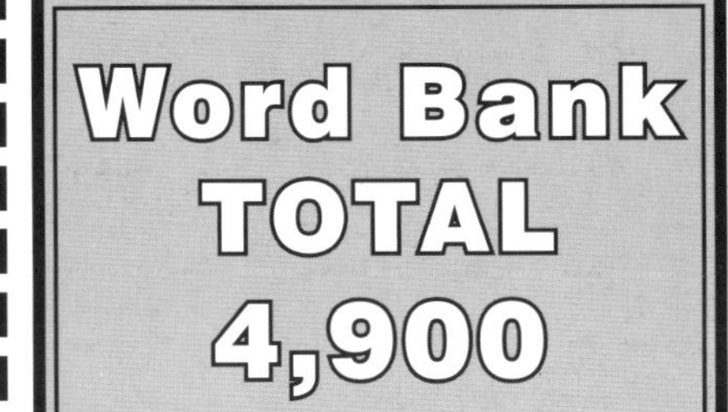

Across

245

3. Straight lines extending from the centre of a circle to its edge.
6. Very cloudy, with no sun showing.
8. Small pieces of coloured paper or dried flowers thrown over the bride and groom at a wedding.
10. Able to be supported or proved with evidence or arguments.
11. Not in accordance with the facts or what is known.
12. A failing, blemish, or flaw.
15. Positioned directly above somebody or something.
17. The gaining back of something lost or taken away.

Across (continued)

18. Requiring a great deal of effort.
19. Amazingly or almost unbelievably great or wonderful.

Down

1. Somebody who plays the piano.
2. A barrier that protects defenders or blocks a route.
4. The pale cool light that shines from the Moon on a clear night.
5. On or over land that is near water.
7. To challenge or question something.
9. To kill or injure a person or animal by squeezing the throat.
13. A horse chestnut, without its spiny casing.
14. Belonging or relating to motherhood, a mother, or mothers in general.
15. Late or after the scheduled time, especially in arriving occurring, or being paid.
16. A diagram used to indicate relationships between two or more variable quantities.

Mystery Letter

Score
20

Across

246

3. Tending to be beneficial or favourable towards somebody or something.
4. Past participle of *'shine'*.
7. To exclude a baptized Christian from taking part in Communion.
12. Small sweet food items such as chocolate bars, mints, and toffee.
13. Boring because of being long, monotonous, or repetitive.
14. Rounded and swollen-looking.
15. Carried out in a methodical and organized manner.
16. Large, solid, and heavy.

Across (continued)

18. Allowing light to pass through with little or no interruption or distortion so that objects on the other side can be clearly seen.

Down

1. The ability or power to bear prolonged exertion, pain, or hardship.
2. About whom or which little is known or explained.
5. Skilled in practical or scientific subjects.
6. A preposition or adverb indicating the direction, destination or position of somebody or something.
8. The possibility or means of entering or approaching a place.
9. The surround of a fireplace, especially its projecting top.
10. Not straightforward, sincere, and honest in or about your intentions or motives.
11. Abnormally active, restless, and lacking the ability to concentrate for any length of time.
14. A narrow desk with a writing surface and drawers.
17. The part of a large vehicle where the driver or operator sits.
19. A member of a religious community of women.

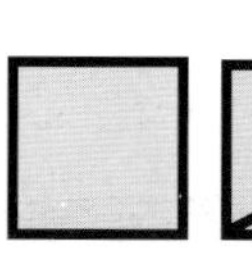

Mystery Letter

Score

20

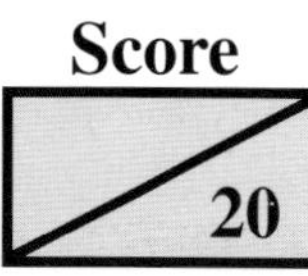

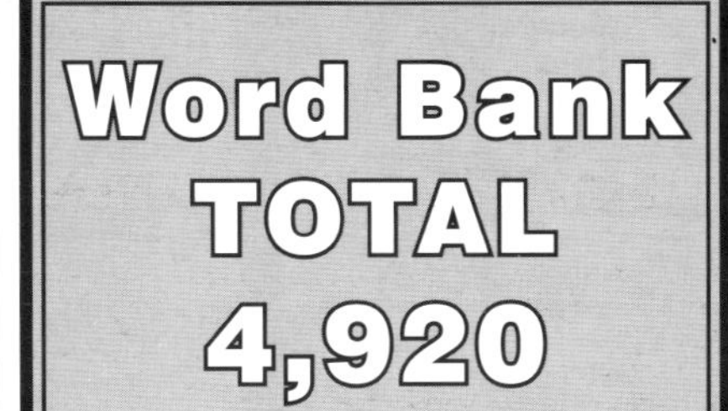

Exercise 246a

1) She put the letters behind the ornament on the ____________________ .

2) He hailed a horse-drawn ________ and asked the driver to take him to Claridge's.

3) The residents gave the new arrivals a ____________ welcome to their street.

4) Rehearsals can be ______________ but they should guarantee a fine performance.

5) Experts with ______________ expertise were needed to solve the complex problem.

6) He could see the car coming: its headlights __________ brightly through the trees.

7) "May we have some __________ floss when we visit the end of the pier?"

8) He has a red, ______________ nose caused by heavy drinking over many years.

9) They went to the ______________ de change to purchase some Euro.

10) It is a __________________ illness about which little is known.   **Score** ⟋ 10

Exercise 246b

11) The route was ______________ : they often thought that they had taken a wrong turn.

12) After he stopped exercising, he gained a ______________ amount of weight.

13) She feared the Church would ____________________ her brother for heresy.

14) Running a marathon severely tested his ________________ but he completed the course.

15) They considered the possible causes one at a time, in a ________________ way.

16) The novitiate took her final vows and became a ________ , to be known as 'Sister Mary'.

17) His motives are completely ________________ and totally selfish.

18) He was ________________ and never seemed to tire of running around excitedly.

19) She entered her password to ____________ the computer network.

20) "Remember! It is similar ______ and different *from*."   **Score** ⟋ 10

Exercise 247a

1) She made a ___________________ of the completed form before posting it.

2) The highwayman waited for another opportunity to ____________ a traveller.

3) The police officer give to the court a simple, ____________ account of the incident.

4) The ___________________ was busy and all of the exercise equipment was in use.

5) He took his time to ________________ a plan: he could not afford any mistakes.

6) The ________ squirrel has contributed to the decline of the indigenous red squirrel.

7) "He never lacks ___________________ and is always eager to complete any challenge."

8) She sprinkles ________________ onto her soups and salads to add texture and flavour.

9) The rocket's ________________ system malfunctioned and it plunged into the sea.

10) One thousand litres of water have about one ____________ of mass. **Score** / 10

Exercise 247b

11) The ________________ Act of 1940 enabled enemy spies to be prosecuted and executed.

12) Honey ____________ grows on living trees and on dead and decaying woody material.

13) He is engrossed by his video game and ________________ to everything else.

14) The circulation returned to her hand after minutes of ________________ rubbing.

15) A card from the Queen arrived for their golden wedding ___________________ .

16) *Elaphrosaurus* was a ___________________ dinosaur of the late Jurassic period.

17) *Judogi* is the name for the traditional costume used for ________ practice and competition.

18) She had to learn complex chemical ________________ for her exam.

19) The latest findings ______________ with those of the original report.

20) The bold designs ________________ the viewer's imagination. **Score** / 10

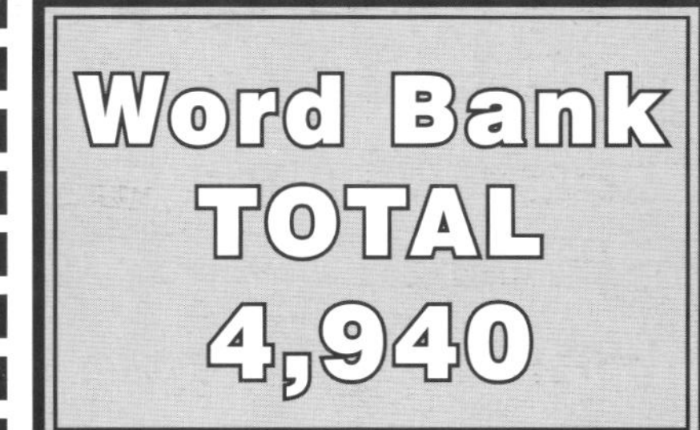

Across

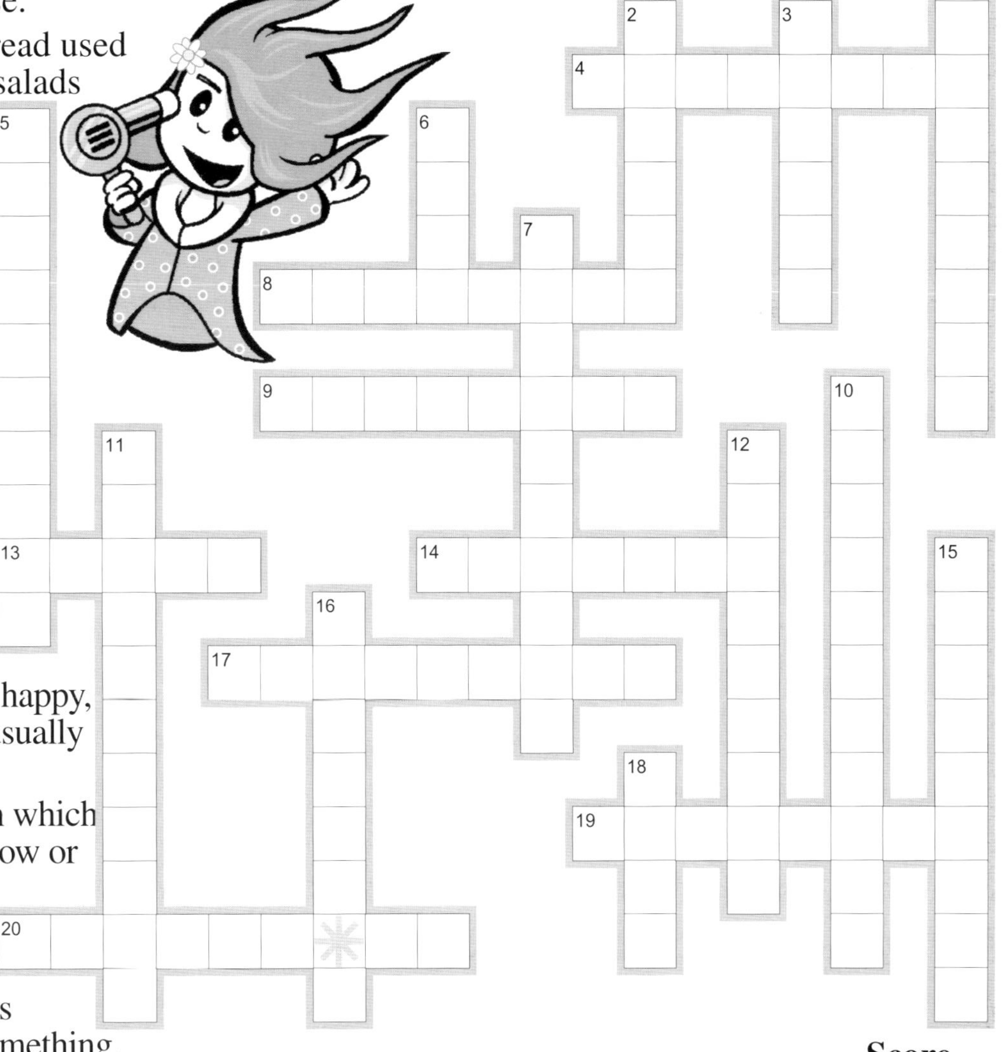

4. Leadership or direction.
8. Extremely strong and active, physically and mentally.
9. A disagreement or clash between ideas, principles, or people.
13. A unit of weight equal to 1,000 kg.
14. Adhering strictly to the basic meaning of an original word or text without further elaboration or interpretation.
17. A copy of something printed, written, or drawn that is produced almost instantly by a photographic process in a machine designed for the purpose.
19. Small pieces of fried bread used as a garnish for soups, salads and other dishes.
20. To draw something up carefully and in detail.

Down

1. Betrayal or deceit.
2. A spore-producing organism such as mildews, moulds, mushrooms, rusts, smuts, and yeast.
3. To lie in wait for somebody.
5. To make somebody feel happy, excited, and more than usually vigorous and alive.
6. A Japanese martial art in which opponents attempt to throw or pin each other, or hold each other in a lock.
7. A feeling of interest or enthusiasm that makes somebody want to do something.
10. Feeding mainly on the flesh of other animals.

Down (continued)

11. A date that is observed on an annual basis because it is the same date as a remarkable event in a past year.
12. Unaware of or paying no attention to somebody or something.
15. A hall equipped for physical exercise or physical training of various kinds.
16. Prescribed and more or less invariable ways of doing something to achieve a particular end.
18. The colour of ash or lead.

Mystery Letter

Score / 20

Across

248

3. Behaviour that shows a lack of respect and shameless boldness.
5. A game played by teams on horseback, with players using long-handled mallets to drive a wooden ball into a goal.
6. Uncertain about an outcome or conclusion.
7. Knives, forks, and spoons used for eating.
11. Lower than somebody else in rank or status.
12. A large building in which goods, raw materials, or commodities are stored.
14. An irresistible alluring quality that somebody or something possesses.
16. The grasping of the meaning of something.

Across (continued)

17. A fact or occurrence that can be observed.
18. To behave or think in a socially acceptable or expected way.
19. To make a feature of something more noticeable.

Down

1. A rich cake, usually consisting of several layers held together with a cream filling.
2. Occurring or repeated in cycles.
4. Any tree that has thin leaves (needles) and produces cones.
5. A doctor trained in the treatment of people with mental illnesses.
8. The feeling of being full of happy high spirits and vitality.
9. With six straight sides and six angles.
10. Punishment that is inflicted in return for a wrong.
13. A boat built to operate and travel for long periods underwater.
15. Outside the sphere of scientific knowledge.

Mystery Letter

Score

/20

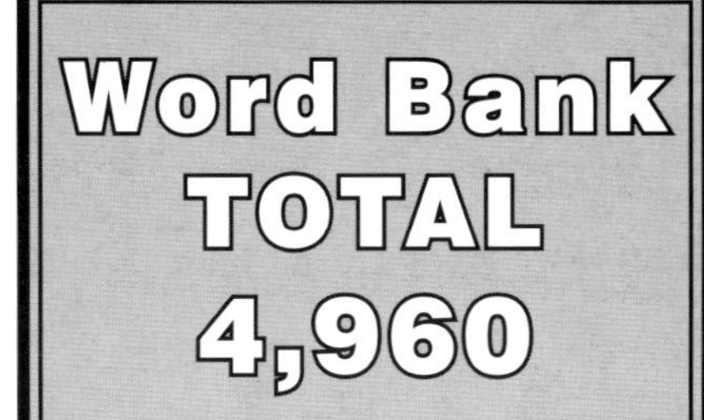

Exercise 248a

1) The _____________________ captain scanned the horizon through the periscope.

2) Her uncle gave the couple a beautiful canteen of _____________ as a wedding present.

3) He wore a white _________ neck sweater under his jacket to protect him from the cold.

4) "The chocolate _______________ looks very rich, so I'll just have a small slice please."

5) Their boisterous behaviour is merely a display of youthful _____________________ .

6) Each gang sought _____________________ for the other's violent acts.

7) A _______________________ test examines a student's understanding of a short text.

8) Ectoplasm is a strange paranormal _______________________ that many scientists refute.

9) There have been many studies into claims to supernatural _____________ powers.

10) " _____________________ the syllable that has the accent over it."

Score / 10

Exercise 248b

11) Education on the risks to health has dissipated the _______________ of smoking.

12) Goods that are subject to import duty are placed in a bonded _____________________ .

13) The soft wood from _________________ trees, such as spruce, is ideal for papermaking.

14) Your _____________________ is astonishing! I have never known such rudeness."

15) Graphite is a six-sided crystal that crystallizes in the _________________ crystal system.

16) _____________ form is a technique of musical construction using a recurring theme.

17) All electrical goods must _________________ to stringent European safety standards.

18) His doctor referred him to a _____________________ to treat his neurosis.

19) She authorized a _____________________ to deputize for her during her absence.

20) The thesis is based on several _______________ theories.

Score / 10

Exercise 249a

1) The activists asked consumers to _______________ the company and its fur products.

2) The organization of food distribution was _____________ and many went without.

3) The sides of a meniscus fall due to _______________ action within a container.

4) The delicate wings are so _________________ they are almost transparent.

5) Success seems unlikely, but nothing is impossible and he remains ___________________.

6) In her bedsitter, the __________ is used as a sofa during the day and as a bed by night.

7) The __________________ exploded high in the air in a starburst of brilliant colour.

8) Six __________________ ships, full of convicted criminals, left Plymouth for Australia.

9) There is a _________ in his argument that can be exploited by his opponents.

10) "He was dressed entirely in _____________ : blue from head to toe!" **Score** ◻ 10

Exercise 249b

11) He sought _______________________ for the injuries he sustained in an accident at work.

12) The headache from her _________________ was intense: she felt sick and debilitated.

13) They watched the aircraft _________ to the stand where it discharged its passengers.

14) Sir Steve Redgrave achieved a great ________ winning five successive Olympic gold medals.

15) He was threatened with _________________ from school if his bad behaviour continued.

16) The baby drank her entire feed: not even a ________________ remained in the bottle.

17) "A car like that is an ___________________________ in today's economic climate!"

18) Peter Bird was __________________ to be the first to row solo across the Pacific Ocean.

19) He knew she was at home: he could see her _________________ on the curtain.

20) As the water rose, they _______________ higher ground. **Score** ◻ 10

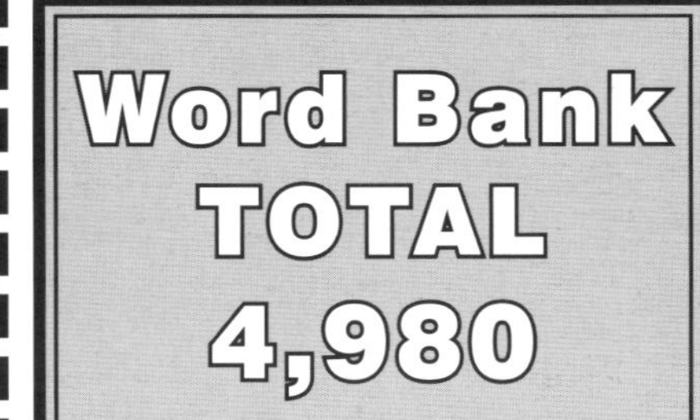

Across

249

1. The act of preventing something or somebody from entering or participating.
5. A unit of volume equal to one thousandth of a litre.
9. Completely disordered and out of control.
12. An outline of somebody or something filled in with black or a dark colour on a light background.
15. An extremely narrow thin-walled blood vessel.
16. A recurrent, throbbing, very painful headache.
17. Allowing light to pass through, but only diffusely, so that objects on the far side cannot be clearly distinguished.

Across (continued)

18. To pay another for doing work or for performing a service.
19. A remarkable act or achievement involving courage, skill, or strength.

Down

1. Excessive or wasteful spending of money.
2. Tending to take a hopeful and positive view of future outcomes.
3. Having a strong desire to be successful in life.
4. A defect in an object that makes it imperfect or less valuable.
6. Past tense of *'seek'*.
7. To cease or refuse to deal with something as a protest against it.
8. A package of manufactured chemicals designed to make a loud and brilliant explosion when lit.
10. A hard-wearing cotton cloth that is typically used to make jeans.
11. A bed with no headboard or footboard.
13. To carry people or goods from one place to another.
14. A car whose driver is paid to transport passengers, typically for short distances.

Don't forget to go back to page **38** and complete **Kate's Mystery Word.**

Mystery Letter

Score

/ 20

Book Eleven Word List

abbey	capable	cowardly	energy
absence	capillary	create	enormous
accentuate	carnivorous	creation	essay
access	cartridge	creditable	estuary
accommodation	cathedral	crime	evaporate
acquaint	cenotaph	croutons	evidence
acquaintance	challenge	crystal	exceeding
acquainted	chaotic	cuckoo	excitement
acquire	character	cutlery	exclusion
advertise	chess	cyclic	excommunicate
advertisement	Chinese	dainty	execute
albatross	chisel	decision	exhausted
ambition	choir	defect	exhilarate
ambitious	circumstance	definite	explosion
angle	circus	denim	extravagance
angling	civil	deposit	extravagant
anniversary	civilized	description	extreme
annoy	cleanliness	design	extremely
annoyed	coconut	despair	exuberance
antiseptic	college	despise	fabulous
apparent	collie	destination	faithful
application	combination	destitute	famine
approve	commence	destruction	fanatical
aqualung	commit	detail	fatal
architect	complaint	develop	feat
arguable	compliment	devious	filleting
arrival	composer	difference	firework
assassinate	comprehension	digest	flavour
assistance	computer	digestion	flaw
athletic	comrade	disappoint	formulae
authoress	concern	dissolve	formulate
bachelor	conclusion	distribute	fossil
badminton	confetti	divan	fragrant
bankrupt	conflict	division	freight
barricade	conform	domestic	friendly
bassoon	coniferous	dubious	frigid
beverages	conker	elegant	fungus
boycott	consideration	ellipse	gateau
bulbous	contagious	emergency	generous
burden	contest	emigrant	genuine
bureau	continually	emigrate	glamour
cab	conversation	encouragement	glider
caddy	convert	endeavour	granite
candy	convey	endurance	graph

Book Eleven Word List

gratitude
grey
guarantee
guidance
gymnasium
hand-grenade
hazardous
headgear
heal
heir
heroic
hexagonal
honourable
hosiery
hula-hula
humiliate
humour
hyperactive
ideal
impatience
impatient
impudence
impudent
incident
independent
influence
innocent
inoculation
instruction
insurance
intelligence
intelligent
intention
interfere
invalid
invention
isles
item
judgment
judo
kitchenette
laborious
ladle
leveret

liable
literal
luxury
magnificent
maintain
majestic
manageable
mantelpiece
margin
marvellous
massive
maternal
medicine
messenger
migraine
millilitre
mischievous
miserable
moccasin
monarch
moonlight
moral
motivation
mould
mourn
muscle
mutiny
mysterious
national
numerous
nun
objection
obliging
oblivious
observatory
obstinate
occasion
occasionally
octagon
offence
offend
offshore
operation
opinion

oppose
opposite
opposition
oppress
optimistic
origin
original
overcast
overcoat
overdue
overhead
overturn
parliament
patient
pattern
peaceable
penalties
pension
pentagon
phenomenon
phone
photocopy
photograph
phrase
physical
pianist
piecemeal
pierce
pilot
pirouctte
pistol
plateau
polo
poncho
portrait
poultry
poverty
practise
presence
pretence
principle
probable
probably
proceed

proclaim
professional
programme
prompter
pronounce
propeller
proteins
provision
provoke
psychiatrist
psychic
pulse
punctual
pursue
pursuit
quaint
quarry
quench
radii
rallies
reasonable
reception
recollect
recommend
recompense
recovery
reference
reflect
rehearsals
release
reliable
remainder
remembrance
reserve
residence
resign
response
reveal
roulette
rumour
sacrifice
salute
sandwich
satisfaction

Book Eleven Word List

scheme
section
seize
sensation
serving
shawl
shield
shipping
shone
shrivel
silhouette
skiing
skyscraper
society
solve
sought
soul
source
Spain
squirrel
strength
strengthen

submarine
subordinate
suitable
supreme
sustain
swollen
symmetrical
systematic
tambourine
taxi
technical
tedious
telegram
telegraph
tenant
tennis
thorough
thriller
thrive
throttle
to
tobacco

toiled
tonne
torrent
tourist
tourniquet
transform
translate
translucent
transparent
transport
traveller
treachery
trekking
tremor
triangle
trifle
tripod
trophy
tropics
type
typewriter
tyrant

ukelele
umpire
unaccompanied
unaffected
untrue
vacant
vapour
variety
vengeance
ventilation
vigorous
violence
volume
vulgar
waitresses
warehouse
waylay
wholly
wig
witness
Yen
yield

Congratulations!

You have now learnt to spell **4,980** words, know what they mean and how to use them in a sentence.

Now move on to **Book 12** to learn lots more words to add to your word bank total.

Answers

Exercise 228a
1) conversation
2) photograph
3) intention
4) Telegram
5) phrase
6) principle
7) national
8) choir
9) combination
10) fatal

Exercise 228b
11) ventilation
12) telegraph
13) Cathedral
14) domestic
15) physical
16) punctual
17) section
18) consideration
19) continually
20) sensation

Crossword No. 228

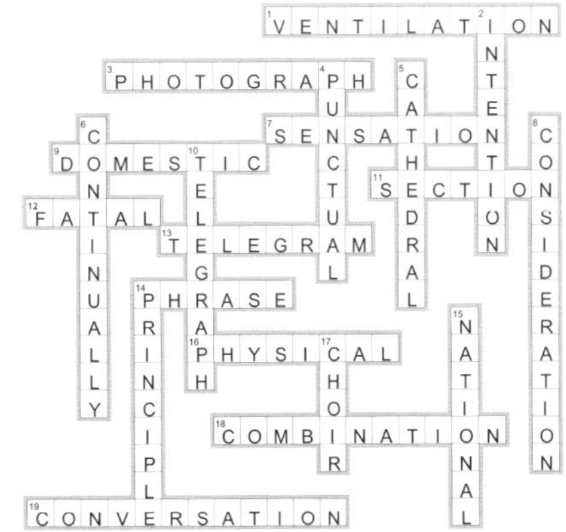

Letter = S

Exercise 229a
1) heroic
2) majestic
3) seize
4) pilot
5) miserable
6) tropics
7) tyrant
8) item
9) extravagant
10) pistol

Exercise 229b
11) circumstance
12) assistance
13) remembrance
14) vacant
15) elegant
16) athletic
17) insurance
18) tenant
19) ideal
20) fragrant

Crossword No. 229

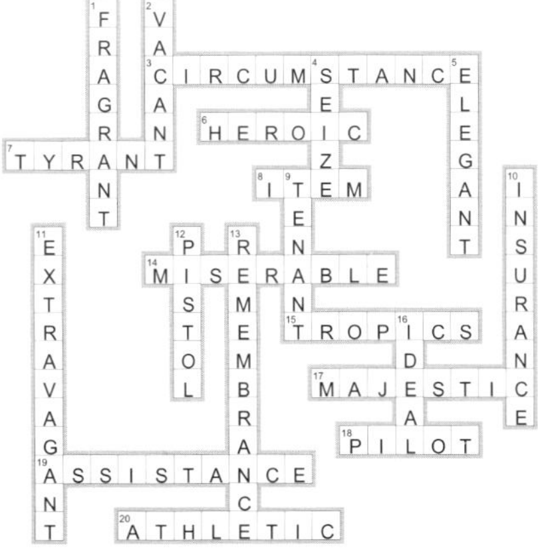

Letter = C

Exercise 230a
1) probable
2) influence
3) description
4) cleanliness
5) witness
6) angle
7) convert
8) probably
9) destruction
10) reasonable

Exercise 230b
11) liable
12) energy
13) concern
14) trifle
15) reliable
16) despair
17) muscle
18) capable
19) despise
20) convey

Crossword No. 230

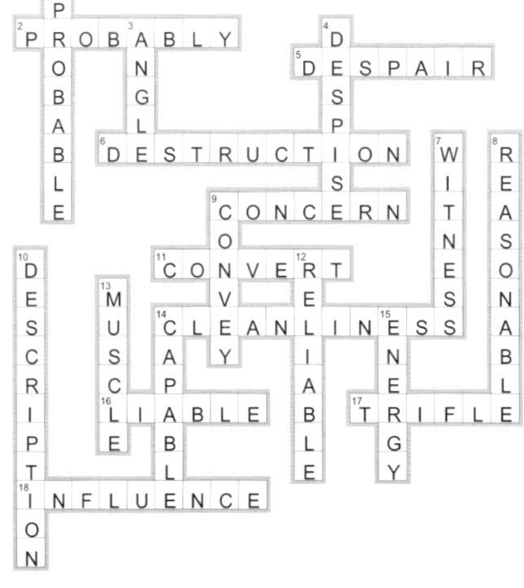

Letter = B

Answers

Exercise 231a

1) Circus
2) absence
3) definite
4) ambition
5) genuine
6) presence
7) crime
8) reference
9) pretence
10) umpire

Exercise 231b

11) instruction
12) granite
13) objection
14) reception
15) evidence
16) salute
17) residence
18) medicine
19) famine
20) satisfaction

Crossword No. 231

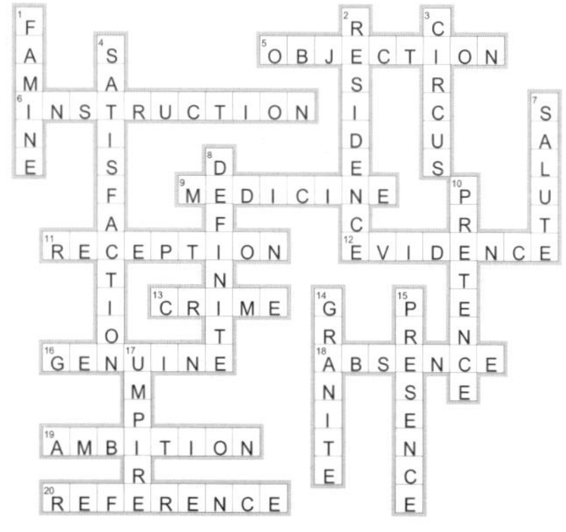

Letter = N

Exercise 232a

1) disappoint
2) swollen
3) abbey
4) acquaint
5) detail
6) distribute
7) burden
8) acquaintance
9) execute
10) strength

Exercise 232b

11) gratitude
12) acquainted
13) develop
14) deposit
15) destitute
16) pattern
17) luxury
18) strengthen
19) acquire
20) volume

Crossword No. 232

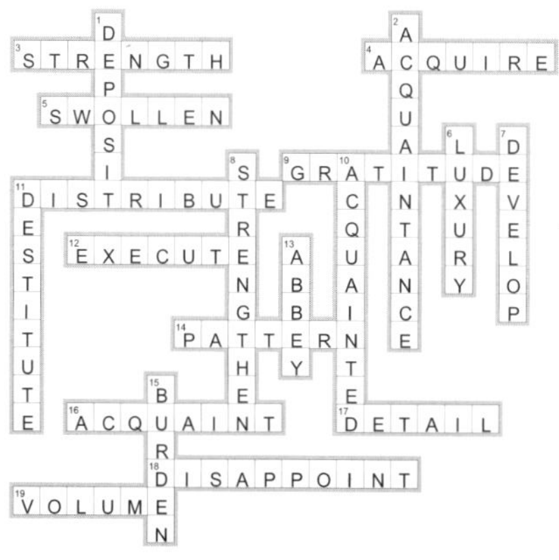

Letter = E

Exercise 233a

1) application
2) reveal
3) approve
4) oppose
5) traveller
6) College
7) opposition
8) messenger
9) offend
10) response

Exercise 233b

11) flavour
12) design
13) reflect
14) remainder
15) opposite
16) release
17) oppress
18) challenge
19) reserve
20) resign

Crossword No. 233

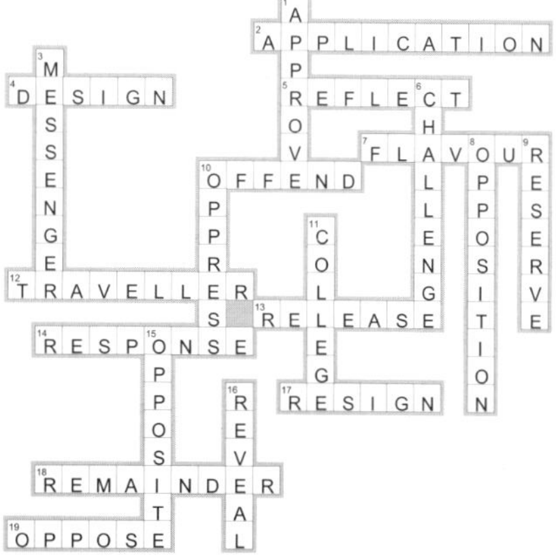

Letter = A

Answers

Exercise 234a
1) advertisement
2) occasionally
3) invalid
4) independent
5) vapour
6) yield
7) enormous
8) pierce
9) generous
10) practise

Exercise 234b
11) rumour
12) excitement
13) impudent
14) innocent
15) mischievous
16) shield
17) numerous
18) marvellous
19) advertise
20) occasion

Exercise 235a
1) invention
2) heir
3) mould
4) frigid
5) proclaim
6) operation
7) patient
8) provoke
9) civil
10) poultry

Exercise 235b
11) digest
12) impatience
13) pronounce
14) civilized
15) proceed
16) impatient
17) commit
18) opinion
19) digestion
20) soul

Exercise 236a
1) tobacco
2) complaint
3) dissolve
4) solve
5) shipping
6) division
7) endeavour
8) annoy
9) decision
10) poverty

Exercise 236b
11) pension
12) recommend
13) recollect
14) annoyed
15) wholly
16) comrade
17) conclusion
18) humour
19) commence
20) provision

Crossword No. 234

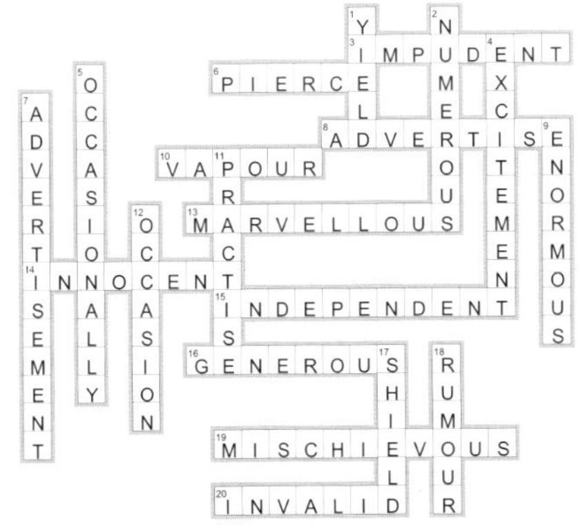

Letter = O

Crossword No. 235

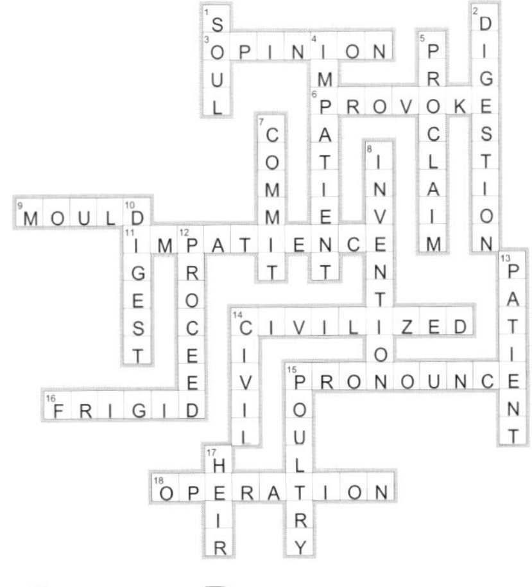

Letter = D

Crossword No. 236

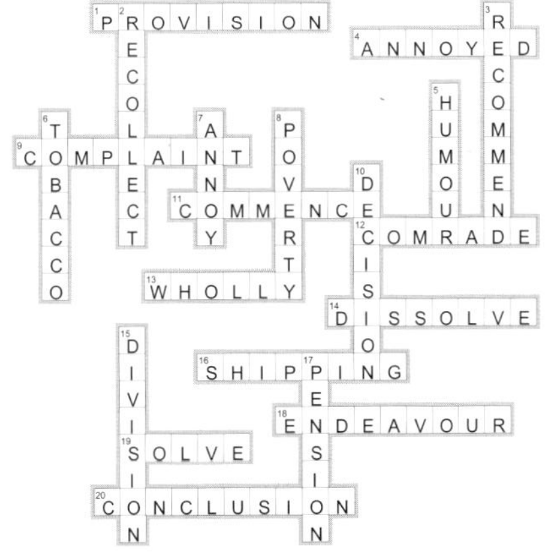

Letter = P

At the Birthday Party

1. SLICE	2. BALLOONS	3. PATCH	4. DONKEY	5. LEMONADE
6. JELLY	7. PRESENTS	8. FAIRY CAKE	9. CARD	10. ZIP FASTENER
11. DOLL	12. CANDLES	13. ECLAIR	14. BLINDFOLD	15. ENTERTAINER

On the Canal

1. LOCK	2. RAILING	3. BAIT	4. LANDING NET	5. BOW
6. PAINTER	7. LIFEBELT	8. FENDER	9. REEL	10. STERN
11. FISHING ROD	12. DUCK	13. NARROWBOAT	14. LOCK KEEPER	15. HAMPER

Answers

Exercise 237a

1) transform
2) quench
3) margin
4) sandwich
5) mutiny
6) Spain
7) variety
8) quaint
9) programme
10) original

Exercise 237b

11) translate
12) dainty
13) arrival
14) character
15) society
16) create
17) sacrifice
18) origin
19) crystal
20) moral

Crossword No. 237

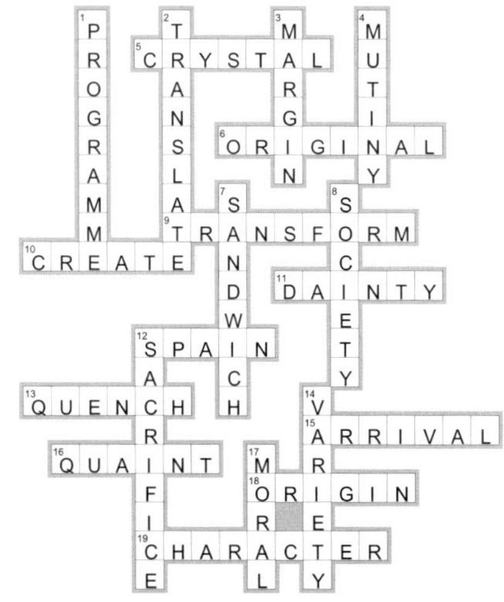

Letter = H

Exercise 238a

1) emigrate
2) manageable
3) extremely
4) creditable
5) pursuit
6) intelligent
7) Chinese
8) supreme
9) obstinate
10) suitable

Exercise 238b

11) mourn
12) peaceable
13) extreme
14) pursue
15) scheme
16) creation
17) interfere
18) honourable
19) emigrant
20) source

Crossword No. 238

Letter = O

Oliver's Page of Knowledge

1. Joseph Foljambe
   Plough.
2. Laszio Biro
   Ballpoint Pen.
3. Charles Babbage
   Computer.
4. Gustaf Erik Pasch
   Safety Match.
5. Frank Whittle
   Jet Engine.
6. James Hargreaves
   Spinning Jenny.
7. Trevor Bayliss
   Clockwork Radio.
8. Robert William Thomson
   Pneumatic Tyre.
9. Rudolph Diesel
   Diesel Engine.
10. John Logie Baird
    Television.

Answers

Exercise 239a

1) judgment
2) magnificent
3) squirrel
4) typewriter
5) sustain
6) intelligence
7) quarry
8) compliment
9) Parliament
10) maintain

Exercise 239b

11) torrent
12) essay
13) apparent
14) vulgar
15) incident
16) portrait
17) offence
18) type
19) difference
20) thorough

Exercise 240a

1) exhausted
2) angling
3) destination
4) hand-grenade
5) badminton
6) authoress
7) chisel
8) ellipse
9) isles
10) filleting

Exercise 240b

11) evaporate
12) faithful
13) cuckoo
14) hosiery
15) guarantee
16) accommodation
17) hazardous
18) freight
19) cowardly
20) humiliate

Exercise 241a

1) beverages
2) Pentagon
3) pirouette
4) waitresses
5) hula-hula
6) obliging
7) Observatory
8) tambourine
9) exceeding
10) toiled

Exercise 241b

11) ladle
12) coconut
13) fanatical
14) rallies
15) tennis
16) Chess
17) assassinate
18) emergency
19) octagon
20) collie

Crossword No. 239

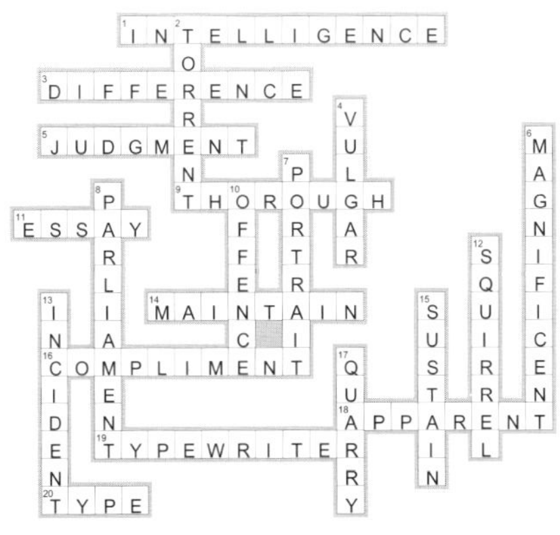

Letter = J

Crossword No. 240

Letter = R

Crossword No. 241

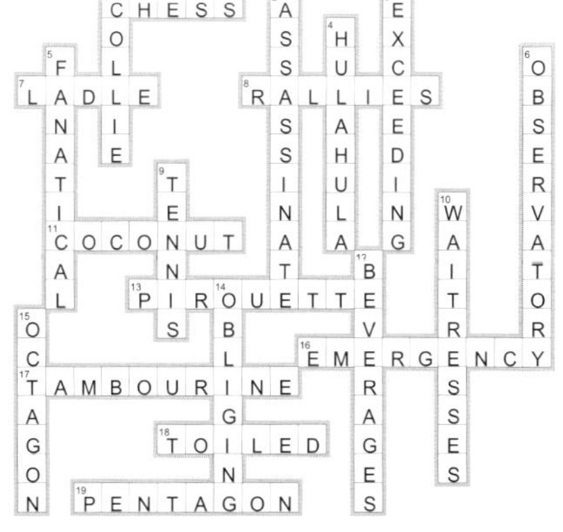

Letter = S

In the Garage Workshop				
1. HOIST	2. MECHANIC	3. SCREWDRIVER	4. EXHAUST	5. TOOLBOX
6. SPANNER	7. HEATER	8. BATTERY	9. BONNET	10. CHAIN
11. CYLINDER	12. SPARK PLUG	13. JACK	14. AXLE STAND	15. WHEELS

In the Butcher's Shop				
1. TURKEY	2. JOINTS	3. SAUSAGES	4. SAW	5. PASTIES
6. SLICER	7. CASH REGISTER	8. SCALES	9. BUTCHER	10. MINCER
11. CHOPS	12. BURGERS	13. PIES	14. KNIVES	15. CLEAVER

Answers

Exercise 242a

1) rehearsals
2) kitchenette
3) skyscraper
4) piecemeal
5) prompter
6) Triangle
7) penalties
8) unaffected
9) wig
10) cartridge

Exercise 242b

11) poncho
12) tripod
13) caddy
14) inoculation
15) albatross
16) Proteins
17) plateau
18) symmetrical
19) tourist
20) Yen

Exercise 243a

1) unaccompanied
2) bankrupt
3) roulette
4) heal
5) contagious
6) professional
7) glider
8) shrivel
9) ukelele
10) leveret

Exercise 243b

11) shawl
12) encouragement
13) tourniquet
14) tremor
15) antiseptic
16) trekking
17) skiing
18) Cenotaph
19) serving
20) pulse

Exercise 244a

1) propeller
2) composer
3) thriller
4) bachelor
5) bassoon
6) thrive
7) architect
8) estuary
9) computer
10) overcoat

Exercise 244b

11) monarch
12) trophy
13) violence
14) moccasin
15) phone
16) explosion
17) aqualung
18) overturn
19) fossil
20) headgear

Crossword No. 242

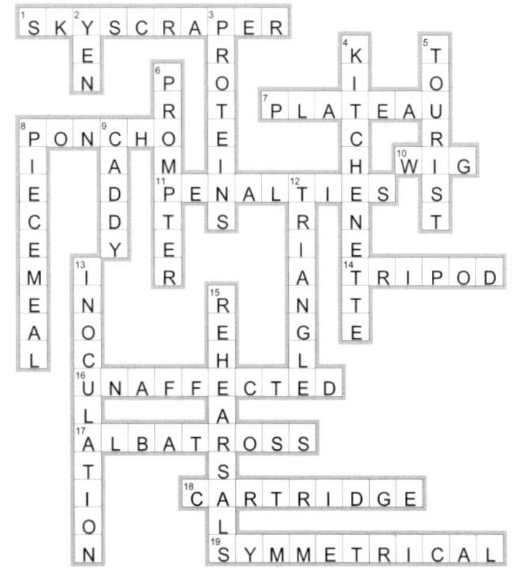

Letter = U

Crossword No. 243

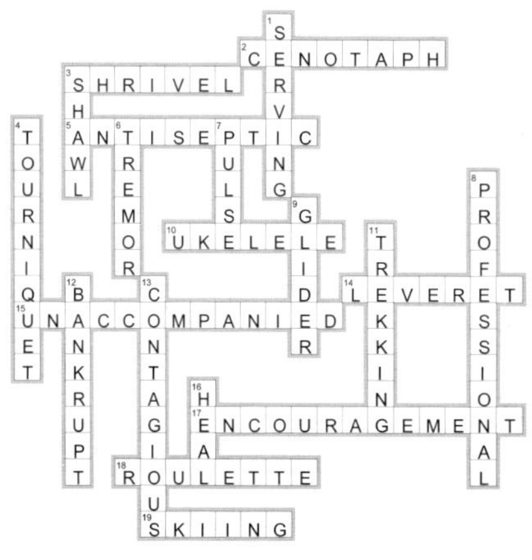

Letter = P

Crossword No. 244

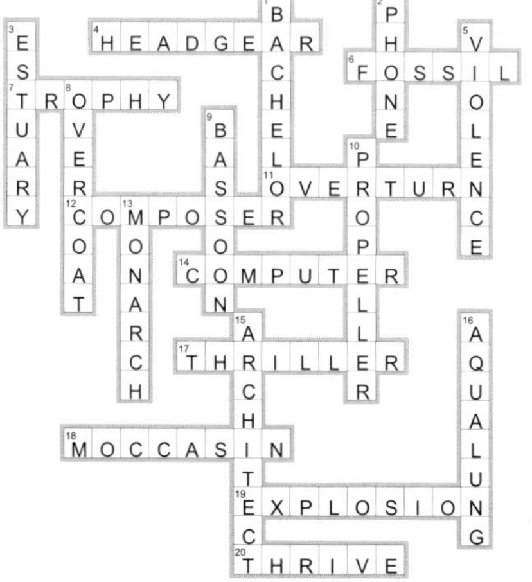

Letter = M

Answers

Exercise 245a

1) offshore
2) conker
3) overdue
4) barricade
5) overcast
6) recovery
7) throttle
8) maternal
9) fabulous
10) defect

Exercise 245b

11) radii
12) contest
13) overhead
14) confetti
15) arguable
16) graph
17) laborious
18) pianist
19) moonlight
20) untrue

Crossword No. 245

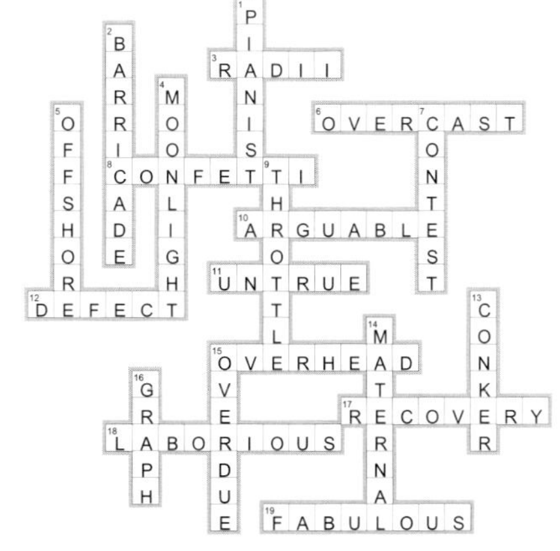

Letter = T

Exercise 246a

1) mantelpiece
2) cab
3) friendly
4) tedious
5) technical
6) shone
7) candy
8) bulbous
9) bureau
10) mysterious

Exercise 246b

11) devious
12) massive
13) excommunicate
14) endurance
15) systematic
16) nun
17) transparent
18) hyperactive
19) access
20) to

Crossword No. 246

Letter = O

Exercise 247a

1) photocopy
2) waylay
3) literal
4) gymnasium
5) formulate
6) grey
7) motivation
8) croutons
9) guidance
10) tonne

Exercise 247b

11) Treachery
12) fungus
13) oblivious
14) vigorous
15) anniversary
16) carnivorous
17) judo
18) formulae
19) conflict
20) exhilarate

Crossword No. 247

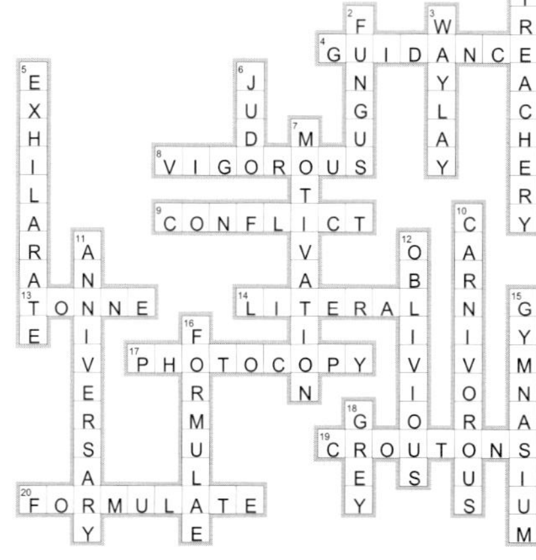

Letter = A

Answers

Exercise 248a

1) submarine
2) cutlery
3) polo
4) gateau
5) exuberance
6) vengeance
7) comprehension
8) phenomenon
9) psychic
10) Accentuate

Exercise 248b

11) glamour
12) warehouse
13) coniferous
14) impudence
15) hexagonal
16) Cyclic
17) conform
18) psychiatrist
19) subordinate
20) dubious

Crossword No. 248

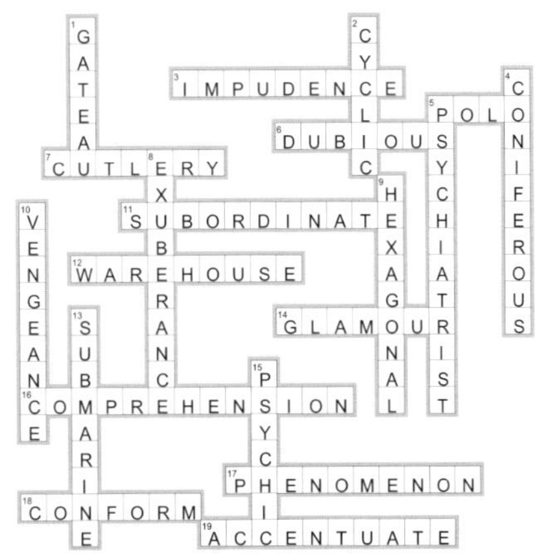

Letter = C

Exercise 249a

1) boycott
2) chaotic
3) capillary
4) translucent
5) optimistic
6) divan
7) firework
8) transport
9) flaw
10) denim

Exercise 249b

11) recompense
12) migraine
13) taxi
14) feat
15) exclusion
16) millilitre
17) extravagance
18) ambitious
19) silhouette
20) sought

Crossword No. 249

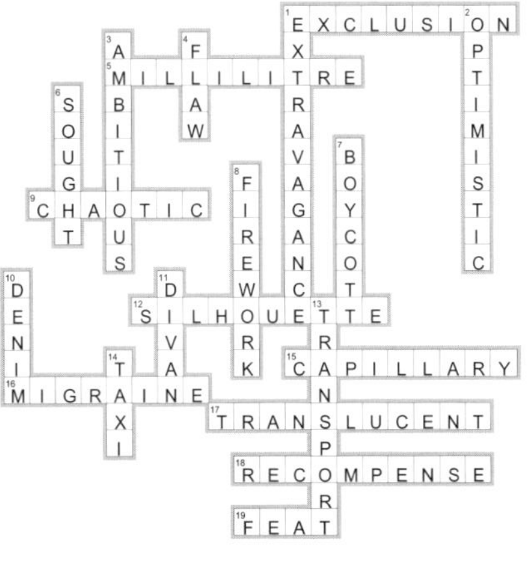

Letter =C

PROGRESS CHARTS

Scores

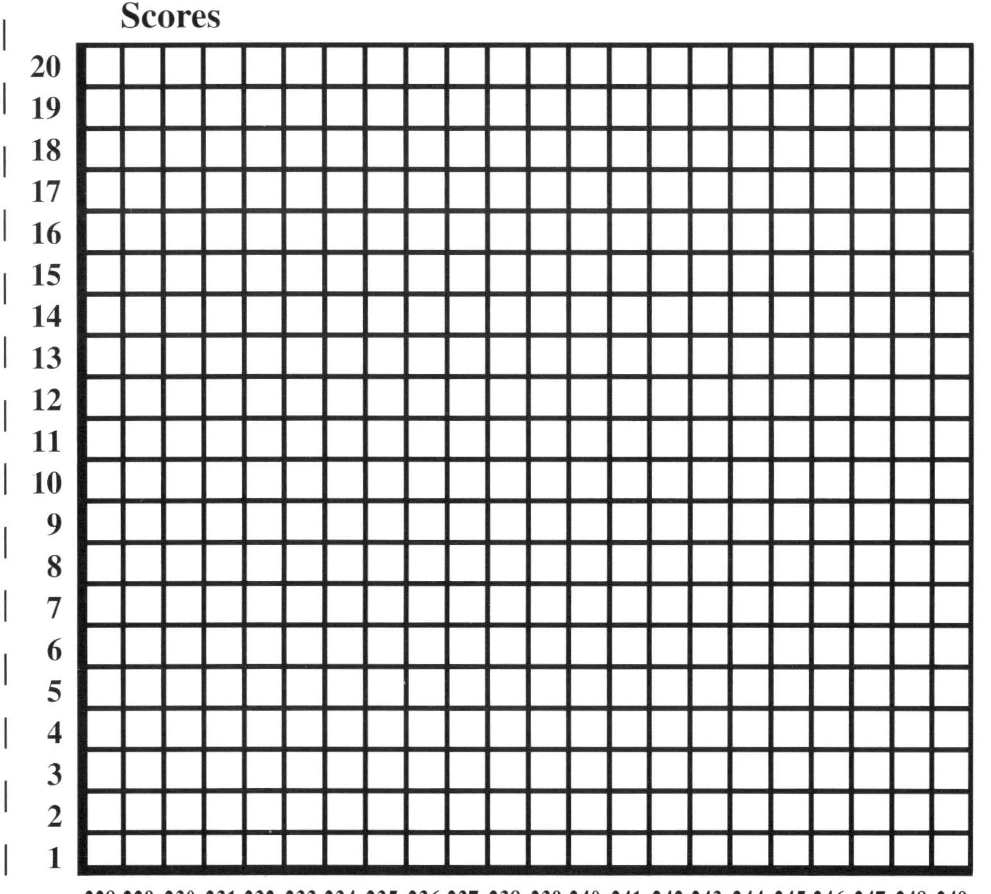

Exercises

Shade in your score for each exercise on the graph. Add them up for your total score out of 440. Ask an adult to work out the percentage.

Total Score

Percentage

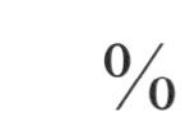

% **A**

Scores

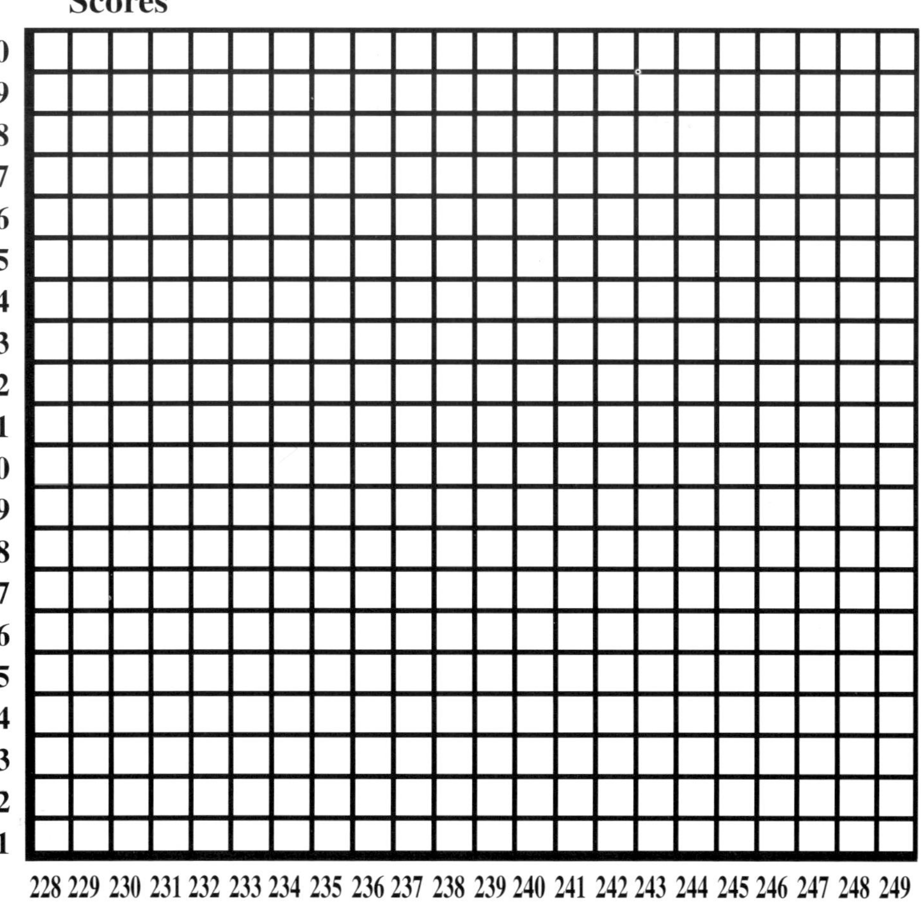

Crosswords

Shade in your score for each crossword on the graph. Add them up for your total score out of **440.**

Total Score

Percentage

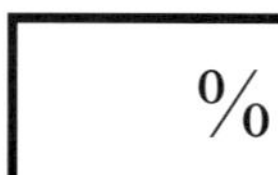

% **B**

For the average percentage add %A and %B and divide by 2.

Overall Percentage

%

CERTIFICATE
OF
ACHIEVEMENT
(Eleventh)

This certifies ....

has completed **Spelling and Vocabulary Book Eleven** successfully.

Overall Percentage
Score Achieved

%

Comment...

....

Signed ....
(Teacher/parent/guardian)

Date ....